# PINA BAUSCH

*dance, dance, otherwise we are lost*

Marion Meyer

# PINA BAUSCH

*dance, dance, otherwise we are lost*

Translated by Penny Black

OBERON BOOKS
LONDON

WWW.OBERONBOOKS.COM

First published in the English language in 2017 by Oberon Books Ltd
521 Caledonian Road, London N7 9RH
Tel: +44 (0) 20 7607 3637 / Fax: +44 (0) 20 7607 3629
e-mail: info@oberonbooks.com
www.oberonbooks.com

Reprinted in 2018

2. überarbeitete und erweiterte Auflage 2/2016

© Bergischer Verlag, © Marion Meyer

English translation copyright © Penny Black, 2017

Foreword copyright © Alistair Spalding, 2017

Penny Black is hereby identified as translator of this work in
accordance with section 77 of the Copyright, Designs and Patents Act
1988. The translator has asserted her moral rights.

This book was selected to receive financial assistance from

Ministerium für Familie, Kinder,
Jugend, Kultur und Sport
des Landes Nordrhein-Westfalen

A catalogue record for this book is available from the British Library.

PB ISBN: 9781783199891
E ISBN: 9781783199907

Cover photo by Walter Vogel

Printed and bound by Replika Press Pvt. Ltd., India.

# FOREWORD FROM ALISTAIR SPALDING, ARTISTIC DIRECTOR, SADLER'S WELLS

There are a handful of artists who have the uncanny ability to bridge the material world and the dream world of the subconscious, of angels and demons. Pina Bausch was one such artist.

She was able to create a world on stage that simultaneously possessed an inner logic and resembled complete chaos. She showed us the full spectrum of human emotion – a world of cruelty, violence, frailty, love and tenderness, mostly seen through the prism of the relationship between men and women.

At the same time, she invented a whole new mode of theatrical expression, that of Tanztheater, which opened a new realm of possibilities for an art form that had, for the most part, been restricted to the abstraction of contemporary dance or the linear narrative of ballet.

She has left a vast legacy – over forty-six works, many of which are still performed by Tanztheater Wuppertal – and influenced a whole generation of dance and theatre makers. Also, for those of us who were lucky enough to know her personally, she left a mark that will never be erased – that of a beautiful human being who inspired absolute devotion and love from everyone that worked with her, both on and off the stage.

There is a photo of Pina in my office at Sadler's Wells – she is looking over me, making sure I work as hard as she did in her life. But her presence is also inside me as I move around the world; she is someone who entered my subconscious, as I am sure she has done with many others who knew her.

*Alistair Spalding,*

*London, January 2017*

## FOREWORD FROM ORIGINAL PUBLISHER THOMAS HALBACH

I was preoccupied with the idea for a series entitled *Bergische Monographie* for several years. I discussed a whole host of ideas with friends, binned several of them, and developed others. And now the first volume in the series is here. The aim of the *Bergische Monographie* is to bring different people from the region closer to the reader; people whose personality, whose work and whose presence has brought them into society at large and made a considerable impression upon it.

But who would be the right person for this first volume in the series? A difficult question. Maybe it should be the best known sovereign of the area, Engelbert von Berg, or even the poet and playwright Else Lasker-Schüler? Who could ignore these people in a series entitled *Bergische Monographie*. It soon became clear that we wanted someone whose work and influence continues to resonate globally. And so, it was decided: Pina Bausch would be an excellent choice for this first volume in the series.

To author it I was fortunate enough to get Marion Meyer: as a journalist Meyer has been fascinated with the work of Pina Bausch for many years. But she has also enough distance from Pina Bausch the person to cast a lucid eye over her life.

And she has succeeded in writing a respectful biography. She approaches her subject's life with great sensitivity, from her first attempts to walk right up to her greatest successes, before concentrating on the individual building blocks of her work.

I am particularly delighted with the inclusion of vivid, revealing and intimate interviews with those who worked closely with Pina Bausch: Jo Ann Endicott, Lutz Förster, Dominique Mercy, Thusnelda Mercy and Jean-Laurent Sasportes.

And we should not forget the work of Ernst-Wilhelm Bruchhaus, who has shown endless patience and empathy in compiling a glorious selection of images for this biography.

My thanks go to all of those who have contributed to this work.

*Publisher Thomas Halbach*

*Wipperfürth, October 2012*

# TRANSLATOR'S NOTE

Marion Meyer's biography of Pina Bausch is wonderfully clear, insightful and warm, yet still Meyer is able to view the life, and in particular the career, of Pina Bausch with a detached journalist's eye. It is warm, because Meyer first worked at the theatre section of the Wuppertaler Bühnen, and so had a chance to see performance from the inside. It is insightful, because she continued to follow the career of Pina Bausch from the outside. An ideal combination.

Her biography sets out how Pina Bausch worked, looks at the individual choreographies, and interviews some of the better-known dancers who worked with her over the years.

I say 'set out' because the mechanics of her life and work are one thing, the magic that brought it all together was of course Pina Bausch. I like the fact that although this biography is so clear-sighted, Pina Bausch herself remains an enigma. It was Heiner Müller who first called Pina Bausch a sphinx. A sphinx is a 'mysterious, inscrutable person or thing, especially one given to enigmatic questions or answers'.

I give you Pina Bausch.

*Penny Black*
*London, January 2017*

# CONTENTS

Pina Bausch
dances in
"Danzón"

# AN INTRODUCTION

It was around midday on 30 June 2009 when our editors received the news from Tanztheater Wuppertal. It stated, in a few stark words: 'Pina Bausch died today, five days after being diagnosed with cancer.' Shock. Confusion. Sorrow. Should we write an obituary? That seemed impossible; of course we had nothing prepared, no one could have guessed that the choreographer would die so soon. Pina Bausch and her ensemble had just celebrated the premiere of a new work at the Wuppertal Opera House. She had received the applause on stage in her modest way, smiling gently. Although she had looked stressed, skinny and pale even, one had seen this before following phases of extreme exertion.

And now she had died, aged only sixty-eight years old, no one could really believe it. There had been no time to say goodbye. The people of Wuppertal laid flowers out in front of the opera house and lit candles. The Tanztheater company completed its tour of Poland bravely and professionally before collapsing into collective mourning. It had lost far more than its famous choreographer. Pina Bausch was its soul, the mother of the company. She had held this family together for thirty-six years and had created a new art form: dance theatre.

Pina Bausch revolutionized dance, introducing new theatrical dimensions to it, enriching it through song and acting, bringing in global influences. She had developed a dance language that was understood around the world because of its universal humanity, and as a cultural

Pina Bausch during rehearsals for "Walzer" at the Lichtburg in Barmen, 1982

ambassador she had exported this humanity to countless other countries. Her pieces are timeless; even decades later they have an ability to move. Nearly every year she had presented a new work, initially without a title, as a kind of work in progress. She never felt truly finished with a piece and was apparently rarely satisfied.

She was a restless worker and seldom took breaks or time off. Everything flowed into one – private life, rehearsals, performances, travel. Very little is known of her private life. She never spoke about it and her son, Salomon Bausch, is keeping it that way. But she was always on duty for the Tanztheater. She watched virtually every performance and would give notes afterwards, as uncompromising with herself as with others. She demanded a lot, but received back in equal measure. She was awarded all the prizes going, including the German Dance Prize in 1995, and in 2007 both the Golden Lion of Venice and the Kyoto Prize. She was venerated everywhere, whether Paris or New York, Japan, South America or India.

At the end of each performance, in a ritual carried out every evening, the audience leapt to their feet with standing ovations and rhythmical applause to honour the Tanztheater Wuppertal. This enthusiasm was even evident in response to the weaker pieces. The audience loved their Pina and for this reason would happily travel to Wuppertal. Even today the performances are generally sold out weeks beforehand.

Yet it is difficult to imagine now that this was not always the case. When Pina Bausch first took over the Wuppertal Ballet the audiences would walk out, slamming the doors behind them. Tomatoes were thrown onto the stage and the choreographer received threatening phone calls. The audience wanted to watch the sacred world of *Swan Lake*, not couples fighting and tormenting each other. It took several years before they learned to treasure the new, to recognize the richness represented in Pina Bausch's dance.

She broke new ground with her pieces. She reflected everyday life in short episodes that were sometimes aggressive and brutal, at other times delicate and poetic, but always moving, never unaffecting, because the level of humanity and truth in them was recognizable to all. Ensemble dances interchange with solos, short performed scenes with dance. The painful and disturbing aspects of her early unwieldy pieces were superseded from the 1990s onwards by works in which the dancers delighted the audiences with magical solos, exuding liveliness and *joie de vivre*.

Pina Bausch never differentiated between protagonists and supporting performers; they were all equally important to her. In the earlier pieces the ensemble was used in its entirety; later on came works for selected dancers from the ensemble. But no one was left with little to do. She regularly brought older pieces back into the repertoire, which went hand in hand with elaborate rehearsals and sometimes reassignment of roles.

Many of the dancers from the early days stayed loyal to the choreographer, while some, such as Dominique Mercy and Nazareth Panadero, left the ensemble temporarily. Others, such as Jo Ann Endicott, Mechthild Großmann, Jean Laurent Sasportes or Lutz Förster perform all their roles as guest performers, but on an ongoing basis. That some of them are now over sixty years old does not disturb but instead enriches a dance world that is usually so concentrated on youth. Pina Bausch's dancers bring their own personalities along with them. She proved to have a particular knack when choosing them. It was the characters of the people who came from all over the world to work with her in Wuppertal that interested her. It was never so much about 'how the people move, but what moves them'. Right from the start this philosophy marked both Pina Bausch's choice of dancers and her work.

Pina broached the themes she wanted to tackle by means of persistent questioning. Her dancers responded by talking, playing out short scenes, or dancing. Pina would use these to put together her pieces like a collage. She was always circling around key human themes such as fear, longing, doubt, the search for happiness, the brutality of life, the innocence of childhood in contrast to the merciless word of adults. She took the way human beings experience speechlessness, exploitation, humiliation and dependence and wove them into scenes dealing with the complex duality of men and women. Despite the source material coming from individuals, collectively these scenes reflected the core of human experience. Pina Bausch analyzed the world of relationships with an anatomical precision, with ironic wit and delicate humour. She could get to the heart of things in a revealing, devastatingly honest and funny way, and then condense it all theatrically. She once said that emotionality was very important to her, as well as humanity, which lay at the heart of everything.

'Funny how the lovely things [always] have something to do with movement,'[1] she once declared during a rehearsal. In a rare interview, she described dance as a broad church: 'It can be almost anything. It has to do with a certain consciousness, a certain internal physical stance, with an enormous amount of precision: knowledge, breathing, every detail. It always has something to do with the How. Dance is so many things, even very opposite things.'[2]

Pina Bausch never wanted to explain her work, or to label things that each person could and should experience for themselves. She insisted: 'I will prevent myself from naming them. They are quite clearly visible in all my works. I would have to be a poet in order to intuit them again.'[3] During conversations and interviews she clearly felt uneasy and awkward about summing up her work in words. If she could say everything in words, she once remarked, then she would not have felt the need to choreograph.

Was Pina Bausch a political animal? She never let herself be politically harnessed, nor did she express her opinions directly. Instead, she observed her environment with precision. In her works she analyzed social structure and dependencies and held up a mirror to them. But the result was always open to interpretation; she invited the audience to make up their own minds. Nor did she allow herself to be defined as a feminist, despite her many strong female characters: 'Feminism – perhaps because it has become a fashionable word – well, there I retreat into my snail's shell. Perhaps because it often makes a distinction that I don't find very nice. Sometimes it sounds more like conflict than cooperation.'[4]

What one consistently hears is her love of her work, she described her dancers as 'pearls', and her works as 'children': 'One gave everything. And as with children, one loves them all equally.'[5] She viewed herself as a 'realistic optimist'.[6] She

was cosmopolitan, heartfelt, modest, but then again strict, immoderate and uncompromising, not least towards herself. She was strong and yet uncertain, restless, very precise and never careless.

Heiner Müller called Pina a 'sphinx', baffling, a sage. In her memoir, dancer and long-standing ensemble member Jo Ann Endicott described her as an 'export product, a German trademark, the most respected choreographer in the world, the prizewinner of all prizewinners, the artist of the century,' and an 'icon, a legend, an idol, a heroine, a Madonna. She is very very special'.[8] For dance critic Jochen Schmidt, Bausch was the 'Mother Courage of dance'[9]. She was a myth in her own lifetime, and she had to withstand that pressure and those demands. 'I can't afford to get tired,'[10] she once said. She was always wakeful, always approachable, and always on the move. During a trip to India in 1994, she said, 'There are so many things that I would like to experience, to learn. I would like to learn more. Life is over so quickly.'[11]

# CHILDHOOD AND ADOLESCENCE (1940–1959)

## 'I sense people very strongly'

Pina Bausch's parents ran a small hotel in Solingen. What would have become of her had she taken over their business? It is very difficult to imagine her and her distinguished presence pulling beers behind the bar, or her long arms and delicate hands carrying glasses. Did her parents desire a different life for her? The decision to give her the extravagant name of Philippina might suggest so. It was probably shortened to Pina due to pronunciation problems she had as a child.

Pina Bausch was born in Solingen during the Second World War, on 27 July 1940. At some point a bomb landed near her family home. 'I experienced all of that, when I was still a child,' she said. 'Those sorts of things are in my head. They certainly play a big part. I don't know quite how or in what way, but they surely had an effect.'[1] Concrete images of war are not to be found in her works, although intimations of death and dying occur frequently. In *Viktor* the set design is like a burial pit that is just waiting for a gravedigger to fill it in.

During the war young Pina was sent to stay at her aunt's place in Wuppertal, as apparently the bunkers were bigger there. Her black-and-white dotted rucksack, with her doll's head peeping out, was always packed just in case.

Her father, August Bausch, had been a long-distance lorry driver before he and his wife Anita opened the *Zur Erholung*

restaurant in Solingen's Focherstrasse; the double-fronted Hotel Diegel next door came with it. Today there is nothing left of either building. It was from her father, who wore a shoe size 15½, that Pina inherited her large feet: she herself took a size 8½. As a teenager she prayed that her feet would not continue to grow since it would have signalled the end of her dancing career.

She was the youngest of three siblings, and alongside her brother Roland and her sister Anita, enjoyed a great deal of freedom and was allowed to stay up late at night. 'She was allowed to turn everything upside down,'[2] her mother told Pina's childhood friend Walter Vogel, she went on to say that because she and August ran a busy hotel, 'We had no time for the children. So there was never any pressure on them.' Pina and her friends played in the restaurant garden and here she produced her first short plays. 'We played zoos. Some children had to be animals, others the visitors … We pretended we were famous actors. I was always Marika Rökk.'[3]

Pina, hiding underneath the little tables in the inn, was able to study the guests undisturbed. 'My childhood was not awful. It was very imaginative, in fact. I grew up as the daughter of an inn-keeper. I saw many people come in and out and very early on I learned to observe them. Even as a child I developed a strong sense of my fellow human beings and what was going on in their minds. I sense people very strongly.'[4] And everything that she saw and heard fascinated her: friendship, love, discussions and arguments. 'I think that this really activated my imagination. I was always an observer. I was definitely no great talker. I was rather quiet.'[5]

But she did become more involved in the family business if there was a shortage of staff. When she was twelve years old her father became ill and had to go away for treatment. In his absence, all by herself, she pulled the beers and took care of the guests. It was an important experience for her, 'and lovely' too, as she said later.[6] Guests at the restaurant included people from the nearby theatre. 'I was always storming through the restaurant,' she said of her younger days, 'and doing a handstand against the wall and things – I don't remember any more than that, it's just what people told me. And they thought that I was very flexible and should go to a children's ballet group.'[7]

And so, at the age of five, Pina entered the world of children's ballet. She was full of curiosity, without knowing what was expected of her. 'I went along and I tried to do what the others were doing. I can somehow remember that we had to lie on our stomachs and put our legs onto our heads backwards, and then this woman said, "But you are like a contortionist."' This comment apparently impressed little Pina greatly, although she also felt slightly embarrassed: 'Now it sounds very stupid, but somehow I was over the moon that someone had praised me. As the daughter of an inn-keeper you just get on with things; you are sort of always alone. There is no family life.'[8] Her parents were proud of her but they hardly ever watched her dance. 'They were never particularly interested,'[9] she said. 'But I did feel very loved. I didn't have to prove anything. They trusted me.' It was probably the best gift her parents could have given her.

Soon after Pina began ballet classes, she landed small parts in the productions as her talent on stage began to be recognized. She said modestly: 'At first there was nothing. I simply went along and was pulled in for the small children's roles, in operettas as a lift-boy or as an I-don't-know-what in a harem, having to wave the fan, or as a newspaper boy, something like that. And I was always very anxious.'[10] Even as a child, overcoming her fear was one of the things that drove her and helped her to continue to develop. Once she said to her dance teacher: 'I can't do that!' The teacher sent her straight home; Pina suffered for weeks. Only after the teacher asked Pina's parents about her did she return to dance lessons. 'After that I never said "I can't do that" again.'[11]

Dance became increasingly important to Pina Bausch. As she explained when accepting the Kyoto Prize in 2007, it was all she wanted to do. 'In dance I could express all those feelings that I could not say with words. So many different moods, so many shades and hues. And that is what it is about: to sustain the richness, not to constrain it, to make the different moods visible and tangible. Our feelings are very precise.'[12]

So from an early age Pina was clear about her chosen career. After graduating in 1955 from the Evangelische Volksschule Ketzberg in Solingen, she received a scholarship to the Folkwangschule in Essen, known today as the Folkwang University of the Arts. She was just fourteen years old. In her first year she travelled every day between Solingen and Essen, until she moved into a room in a boathouse on Lake Baldeney. Even back then the Folkwangschule was famous not only for its dance department but also for its other disciplines, such as visual arts, photography, graphic arts, music and mime. Each discipline enriched the other disciplines. Dance students in the 1950s and 1960s were 'not only inspired by the variety the dance department had to offer, but also by the exchange with their fellow students from the other disciplines. Meetings during breaks in the courtyard, conversations in the refectory with musicians, actors, graphic designers, photographers or sculptors often inspired one's own productions or were the start of joint projects. The Folkwang idea of interaction between the arts was confirmed by these encounters', wrote Patricia Stöckemann in her biography of Kurt Jooss.[13]

These different influences were vital to the way Pina Bausch developed, to her overarching way of thinking, her way of seeing things, how dance, performance and music could intermingle. Later, Pina recalled: 'It played an incredible role because one learnt something from so many different things and was therefore influenced by all of them … also one was astonished. There were so many things, so many ideas that came together … that one worked on together, it made a huge impression on me.'[14]

The foundations for her career were laid by studying with choreographer Kurt Jooss (1901–79), a forerunner to modern dance, the co-founder of the Folkwangschule and founder of its dance studio. 'Jooss himself was very special to me. He had a lot of warmth and humour and an unbelievable knowledge in all possible areas. Through him I really came into contact with music, for example. Before that I only knew hit records from our guest-house that were played on the radio. He became like a second father. His humanity and his vision were the most important things for me. What good fortune to have met him at such a decisive age.'[15]

Not only was this broad groundwork in all dance styles important, but she needed to establish what she wanted to express as a dancer. 'What do I have to say? In what direction do I have to develop myself further? Perhaps it was here that the foundation was laid for my work.'[16]

The students would meet in Café Döllken opposite the Folkwangschule. The owner, Maria Döllken, remembers: 'Pina was always alone and immersed in thought. She

Pina Bausch
and Jean
Cébron
in "Poèm
dansé –
Epave",
1965

scarcely spoke a word. She had a quite fascinating presence – her whole manner obsessed by dance.'[17] Walter Vogel, who was studying photography in Essen at the time, captured much of Pina's early development with his camera – thank goodness, otherwise there would be very little material from this period. Some of his photographs show Pina on stage with Jean Cébron, a sylph-like pale beauty with a strong presence. As her teacher, dancer Cébron was a major influence on the young student: 'He is someone from whom I learnt the most about movement. About being aware of every small nuance of a movement and what and how things happen at the same time in the body, and and and … one had to think so much. One has the feeling one can no longer dance, a difficult lesson.'[18]

Later, in around 1966/7, Walter Vogel persuaded Pina to come into his studio for a photo session. The results are some wonderful black-and-white photographs that show her, variously, as an unapproachable diva in a black dress, as a naked hat model, as a relaxed student, as a childlike student with her hair down, and of course holding a cigarette – later on an indispensable prop in her hand. These photos reveal the beauty of the nascent world star of dance theatre.

'In front of the camera,' said Vogel of Pina Bausch, 'she put on her enigmatic, ambiguous Mona Lisa smile. Her eyes with their indescribable depths reflected a longing for love and to-be-loved.'[19] Offstage Pina Bausch did not place much importance on her appearance: her pale face was mainly make-up free, and her long hair was tied back into a ponytail.

Vogel describes her wearing 'some sleeveless old t-shirt … that hid her femininity and exposed her washboard-flat décolleté and muscular arms".[20] Her trademark uniform of dark men's clothing, wide trousers, baggy pullovers and jackets came later.

Even then she was a night owl. Vogel remembers: 'After all her moodiness during the day, in the evening Pina became the polar opposite, filled with quiet and nonchalance. Pina still had time for evenings in the bars of Baden-Werden and I had the pleasure, whenever the opportunity arose, to spend time in her company. These nights frequently only ended when the chairs were being stacked.'[22] Later on this would continue, and 'Another wine, another little cigarette', a line from the piece *Walzer*, became a catchphrase on such occasions. At the end of these lively evenings spent surrounded by her fellow dancers, Pina Bausch was often the last person to go home.

## FROM NEW YORK TO ESSEN
## AND EARLY CHOREOGRAPHIES

### 'The only reason was that I wanted to dance'
### (1959–72)

Pina Bausch studied at the Folkwangschule for four years
and graduated with a diploma in stage dance and dance
pedagogy. Her crowning moment was receiving the newly-
created Folkwang Prize for Outstanding Accomplishment.
Her teacher Kurt Jooss commented proudly: 'Pina Bausch,
a wonderful girl … won it against the best pianists, cellists,
actors and singers from the whole school. And not one vote
against her – not from the audience or the jury. Although a
large part of that was due to her extraordinary personality, it
was of course also very good for the whole dance department
and we are very happy about it.'[1]

But what should she do now her studies were over?
Kurt Jooss used to run European-American summer

Pina Bausch,
training, 1967

courses in Essen attended by many famous dancers and choreographers, including José Limón, Antony Tudor and Lucas Hoving. All three of them were based in New York, where important new trends for dance were emerging. Pina Bausch attended their classes and wanted to learn more from them – 'I was ravenous to learn and to dance'[2] – so she applied for a scholarship from the German Academic Exchange Service (DAAD) to attend the famous Juilliard School in New York, regarded as the centre of modern dance studies at the time. It would be two and a half years before Pina Bausch came back to Essen.

The time she spent in New York had a powerful effect: like a sponge she absorbed the many cultural influences of life in the melting pot. She was entranced by the unknown. This need for variety and seeing different cultures living side-by-side would influence her throughout her life. 'To have lived in such a city was very important for me. The people, the city, all embody something of now for me, where everything is mixed together, whether that's different nationalities or interests or fashion, everything is just side by side. Somehow I find that incredibly important.'[3] Multicultural

Main building of the Juilliard School, New York

influences were something that she valued in her ensemble, and she treasured travelling back to the city with the Tanztheater. 'I feel a great connection to New York. Actually when I think of New York, I feel something that I don't feel anywhere else, a slight feeling of home, and so, of homesickness.[4]

One can certainly picture the young dancer in 1959: just eighteen years old, perhaps a little naïve and with no English, diving fearlessly into this great adventure. She travelled by ship to New York entirely on her own. 'When I said "goodbye" to my parents, I thought to myself, perhaps we'll never see each other again. That was a very odd feeling.'[5] But her dance colleagues and the Americans welcomed her warmly.

She rented a room on 125th Street, near to the Juilliard School, and was a hard-working and ambitious pupil. Antony Tudor, José Limón, Margaret Craske and Alfredo Corvino all taught at the school. They also all worked at the Metropolitan Opera, and so young Pina went there too, watching many productions, and even dancing in some of Antony Tudor's pieces. She didn't just get to know the music but also other figures such as Paul Sanasardo and Donya Feuer, who invited her into their dance studio and engaged her for the summer break. A friendship developed between the three of them: Pina appeared in pieces by the pair that were performed at the newly-formed New American Ballet. Meanwhile, she formed a duo with Paul Taylor – which would be an important experience for the young dancer.

It soon became clear to Pina that she did not want to leave New York after just one year. A new opportunity arose when Tudor, by then artistic director of the Metropolitan Opera, offered her an engagement. 'Antony Tudor knew that

I thought one year of study was far too short, it went by too quickly. I saw so many things, I was so busy … it was far too early to go back. I really wanted to stay longer, but of course there was the problem of money. I tried very seriously to eat very little so that the year's money, which was really for nine months or one year, could last for two years. So I saved every cent. I went everywhere on foot.'[6]

Wherever she could save, she did, living on 'ice cream and buttermilk … that was my main meal'.[7] She denied herself a comfortable life in order to continue learning, a motivation that in later years drove her towards new encounters. Even at that time, though, this kind of life wore her out. On her return to Germany she was 'pale and emaciated'. Her mother remembered: 'We went to pick her up and I had a real shock.'[8] But Pina wanted to be thinner still: 'I was always listening to my inner self. To my movement. I had the feeling that inside I was getting purer, deeper. Perhaps it was my imagination. But a change did take place. And not only in my body.'[9]

In 1962, when she received a call from Essen, Pina packed her bags and quit New York, even though it was not easy for her to leave. 'That was a very, very difficult period, I wanted both things so much. It was an extremely difficult decision. I was so happy there, everything was going brilliantly for me.'[10] The Folkwangschule became a university in 1963, whilst the Folkwang Ballet, later known as the Tanzstudio, was founded in 1960, and consisted of protégés and professional dancers. At the time the Folkwang Ballet was a kind of frontrunner for modern dance. Pina became a member of the new ensemble

and also appeared as a soloist; when Kurt Jooss' famous ballet *Der grüne Tisch* (The Green Table) was revived in 1962, she played the old mother. It guested at several festivals, including Schwetzingen and Salzburg. Under Jooss, she planned and ran rehearsals for him on several productions, and he gave her responsibility for his new production of Henry Purcell's opera *Fairy-Queen*, which was also performed at the Schwetzingen Festival in 1969.

Pina Bausch and Kurt Jooss, Schwetzingen, 1967

Halfway through the 1960s, Jooss decided to forego guest choreographers, allowing his comrades-in-arms, Jean Cébron and Pina Bausch, more opportunity to choreograph. The two of them found a protective space in Essen where they could experiment and test themselves, and also appear in performances together. In 1968 Bausch created what is generally considered her first choreography; *Fragment* to music by Béla Bartók. On the whole the work went unnoticed because it was only staged within the Folkwang Tanzstudio, nevertheless, she was already developing her own dance language, heading in the direction of dance theatre. She wanted to create something of her own that was clearly different from anything by her role models. 'I had an incredible shyness about copying someone else. I mean, I would never have dreamt of using one of Martha Graham's or Jooss' movements, or anyone else's. So I started to look around for something simply because I didn't want to use a set vocabulary.'[11]

She succeeded more visibly in 1969 with *Im Wind der Zeit* (In the Wind of Time). 'A bold, grand dance tableau in the classical modern dance style',[12] was how critic Jochen Schmidt described it. Pina Bausch was looking for another dance language but was nonetheless still influenced by her tutors. 'I cannot imitate Jooss or Tudor, nor do I want to. It is about the reason why one does something. And I believe both of them were talking about people, perhaps that is the tradition.'[13]

Later on she would frequently emphasize that the motivation to create her own works actually came out of 'being idle', and a desire to dance more herself. 'I would really have liked to express myself differently, but this was not possible. We didn't have much to do; nothing new ever happened, and so it was out of frustration that I thought, I'm going to try to make something for myself. It was not about doing choreography; the simple reason was that I wanted to dance.'[14]

Her self-image as a dancer was vital to her: 'Everything that I do, I do as a dancer, everything, everything! For me that is the form where I can feel, in which I can express myself best, that is the closest to me.'[15] Clearly, classical ballet was not relevant to her form of expression: 'They wanted to make a ballerina out of me, but I never felt comfortable in that field: pointe shoes always felt like boxing gloves. I want to feel my feet as freely as I feel my hands, to feel everything.'[16]

Pina Bausch entered *Im Wind der Zeit* for the Cologne International Choreography Competition in 1969, one of the most important forums for up-and-coming choreographers, and she succeeded in winning first prize against such great names as Gerhard Bohner, Johann Kresnik and John Neumeier. This first acclaimed recognition of her work gained her much attention across the country. In the same year, when Hans Züllig took over as director of the Folkwang Hochschule's dance department, Pina Bausch became a lecturer there whilst at the same time running the Tanzstudio. In 1970 she created *Nachnull* (After Zero), which premiered in Munich, and in which she began to turn away from modern dance and develop her own dance movements. The dancers wore costumes that made them look like skeletons and performed a dark, angular dance of death in an end-of-the-world scenario, as if after a war.

She created short dances such as *Wiegenlied* (Lullaby), which were mainly distinguished by solos that she danced herself and into which she poured great ardour. Her success led to invitations for first guest performances in London, Manchester, Rotterdam and The Hague, which she was happy to accept. Her reputation grew and grew. In 1971,

Pina Bausch
as the Old
Mother in
"Der grüne
Tisch" by
Kurt Jooss,
1966

despite not having a large body of choreographed work, she received a young artist's development grant in theatre and dance from North Rhine-Westphalia. For Pina Bausch this was vindication and encouragement that she was on the right track.

# BEGINNINGS IN WUPPERTAL (1973)

## 'I didn't want to provoke anyone.'

'The Tanztheater would not have existed without Wüstenhöfer.' Pina Bausch knew how much she owed the artistic director of Wuppertal. Arno Wüstenhöfer belonged to that generation of artistic directors who ensure other artists have the best available working conditions but who remain in the background and do not direct. He had great courage and a huge heart, and soon recognized Bausch's unusual talent. It was Ulrich Kaiser, the city councillor in charge of cultural affairs, who first pointed her out to Wüstenhöfer. 'You like grasping hold of nettles,' said Kaiser, 'then I can give you a tip, do you know Pina Bausch?'

Arno Wüstenhöfer, artistic director of the Wuppertal Stages from 1964 to 1977, brought Pina Bausch to Wuppertal

In joint interviews with Bausch and Wüstenhöfer, their mutual empathy and deep understanding for each other is tangible, almost a father-daughter relationship. 'He gave me confidence, protected me, and introduced me to people,'[3] Pina said of him. Subsequently, when there were conflicts between ensemble members during rehearsals for *Blaubart* (Bluebeard), Wüstenhöfer called the dancers in and persuaded them to stay.

But first he had to persuade Pina to come to his three-stage theatre in Wuppertal, which he ran between 1964 and 1977, when in fact she wanted to work in a much freer way and not be tied to a civic theatre. 'What am I to do in a factory like that?' she allegedly said.

Initially Wüstenhöfer invited her to do a small guest choreography. Günter Becker had been commissioned to compose a twenty-four-minute work for which Pina Bausch and Ivan Sertic, then head of the Wuppertal Ballet, should each create a piece. The whole evening was entitled *Aktionen für Tänzer* (1971): Bausch created a satirical dance piece about a girl in a hospital bed, winning over both Wüstenhöfer and the audience.

She was invited back to choreograph for the Wuppertal Ballet, this time for an opera to be directed by Kurt Horres: she created the *Bacchanal* for Richard Wagner's *Tannhäuser*. Despite illness, she rose to the occasion and, as ever, overcame

The opera
house in
Wuppertal-
Barmen
around 1960

PINA BAUSCH

her fears. Pina Bausch: 'I'm not a person who simply gives up,' she said, 'I don't run away when things get difficult, but that is sometimes really hard.'

Wüstenhöfer approached her again, and after some thought, this time she agreed to return as head of Wuppertal Ballet, eighteen months after *Bacchanal*. It was not immediately obvious that this move would mean a new chapter in the history of dance or that it would be written in, of all places, Wuppertal. The beginning was far from harmonious. Her first pieces shocked audiences deeply, and for one particular work she had to be flanked by four people for protection when she entered the auditorium. But shock was not her aim. 'I didn't want to provoke anyone,'[6] she frequently emphasized.

In time, the people of Wuppertal were won over. The company was invited to tour and take part in festivals, recognition of Pina Bausch increased across Germany and abroad, and visitors flocked to Wuppertal's Elberfelder Theater and Barmer Opera House. On her appointment Pina renamed the company the Tanztheater. 'From very early on I wanted to make it clear, so that people did not have the wrong impression. Before me there had been the Wuppertal Ballet, and ballet is tied into classical dance. The term "dance theatre" is very comprehensive but is not necessarily connected to classical ballet. That was very important to me.'

It took some time before she filled this new term of 'dance theatre' with content. During her first three years she created works that were still influenced by Kurt Jooss and America, works which impressed in terms of visual language but remained wedded to tradition. In 1974, she presented *Fritz*, a smaller work that was shown within the framework of a three-part evening that otherwise comprised Jooss' *Der grüne Tisch* and *Rodeo* by the American, Agnes de Mille. A modest start. At the centre of *Fritz* was a young boy, performed by Marlis Alt, 'whose eyes saw a strange world',[8] in Bausch's words. She contrasted a nightmarish story with the fairy tale of someone who set out to overcome their fears. This theme – the unsettling worlds of adults as viewed through the eyes of children – remained a leitmotif in Pina Bausch's work.

Audiences might have been perplexed by *Fritz*, however critics were beginning to recognize the potential of the young choreographer. Jens Wendland in *Die Zeit* expressed mixed feelings, writing that Bausch groped 'part helplessly, part clumsily around in the theatre and only partially understands the business of directing. On the other hand, she comes up with fantastic ideas'.[9] In the *Munich Evening News* Hartmut Regitz said that 'it again demonstrated the extraordinary talent of the artist'.[10]

For Pina Bausch herself, this first work as head of the Tanztheater proved to be an important experience: 'So many different things come together, one doesn't know where it begins and where it is going to, where imagination is pushing it, or reality … in certain ways it was of course an important piece and it helped me to recognize certain things.'[11] She recognized, for example, that she could not allow herself to be pinned down by preconceived concepts and should instead follow her own creative intuition. She noted that 'with those planned-out works, suddenly completely different things interest me, things that have nothing to do with the planning. Gradually it became clear to me that a decision was needed: to follow the plan or to go in a direction where one has absolutely no idea where one might be heading.'[12]

This openness was one of her most successful traits and was reflected in her way of rehearsing, it also contained a considerable artistic risk: there was no framework, no chosen music, no design, no story, just a vague theme that she approached by means of questions to her dancers.

Before Pina Bausch let go of concepts entirely she created full-length versions of the Gluck operas *Iphigenie auf Tauris* (1974) and *Orpheus und Euridike* (1975). Both are regularly performed even now and their timelessness and poetic picture sequences have lost none of their power. Rolf Borzik contributed to the set design for *Iphigenie* and made his first full set design for Bausch with *Orpheus und Euridike*, creating surreal dream landscapes that reflect the inner lives of the characters.

Rolf Borzik had been Pina's companion since they were both students at the Folkwang-Hochschule and, from 1975 through to his early death from leukaemia at the start of 1980, he created all of the Wuppertal Tanztheater's set designs. Pina said of him: 'He studied graphic design. He was a brilliant draughtsman, but also a photographer and painter. And even as a student he invented all sorts of things. For example, he developed a bicycle that you could ride across water. He was

interested in all things technical. He was an unbelievably creative man. He never dreamt that he would become a set designer. In the same way, I never thought of becoming a choreographer.'[13] The Dutch-born designer, with his unusual set designs and costumes, had an enormous impact on the company's style and contributed greatly to the huge success of the pieces. 'Working together was very intense. We would inspire each other,' explained Pina Bausch. 'Anything that came up whilst we were creating a new piece: questions, endeavours, doubts, even moments of despair – we knew we could rely on each other. Rolf Borzik was always present during rehearsals. He was always there. He always supported and protected me. And his imagination knew no end.'[14]

*Iphigenie auf Tauris* was Bausch's first great success and was celebrated by public and critics alike. In the annual survey for the 1975 German Ballet Yearbook, the reviewers hailed the production as the most important German dance event of the year. Whilst the singers in *Iphigenie auf Tauris* still sing at one side of the stage, it is left to the dancers to embody the events; in *Orpheus und Euridike*, meanwhile, the dancers and singers stand on equal terms next to each other at the heart of the story, creating a beautiful duality. The critic Jochen Schmidt wrote in the *FAZ*: 'For this exploration of the inner world Bausch, together with her serendipitous set designer, Borzik, finds images of dance environments and choreographic sequences of great conciseness and aching beauty.'[15]

Pina Bausch's Stravinsky Evening in 1975 was initially in three parts. It consisted of *Wind von West, Der zweite Frühling* (The Second Spring) and *Le Sacre du Printemps* (The Rite of Spring). Only the latter remained in the repertoire and was soon performed in combination with other works (and later still, as a double bill with *Café Müller*). The thirty-minute piece has become a classic. After nearly forty world tours, it is in fact Wuppertal Tanztheater's most performed piece.

In *The Rite of Spring*, the stage is covered with a thick layer of peat. In a series of eruptive and sweeping group dances, Bausch's adaptation tells the story of a sacrifice – wild, merciless, brutal, yet highly-emotional, erotic and sensuous. The Chosen One, recognizable in a red dress, is caught in the middle between the men and women, who dramatically hunt her to death. By the end, all the dancers are coloured brown by a layer of peat and sweat. *The Rite of Spring* was the first, and apart from *Orpheus und Euridike* (2005), the only piece that Bausch revived with another ensemble – in this case, the Opéra Garnier in Paris in 1997. It was not until April 2016 that the Bavarian State Ballet staged *Für die Kinder von gestern, heute und morgen*, marking the first time that another company produced a piece by Pina Bausch.

She was always keen for her programming choices to remain varied: 'I did *Fritz*, but in the same year I also did *Iphigenie auf Tauris*, which was completely different. And then I did Mahler's *Adagio* and, on the same evening, a hit ballet called *Ich bring' Dich um die Ecke*. And then I did *Orpheus und Eurydike* followed by *The Rite of Spring*. I always went with the extreme, always the opposite … a sort of complete back and forth.'[16] She made these choices based on her intuition, which she always heeded. And she was usually right. She created two pieces per season, a feat that underlines her extraordinary creativity and perhaps, in the early years, an ambition to prove her doubters wrong.

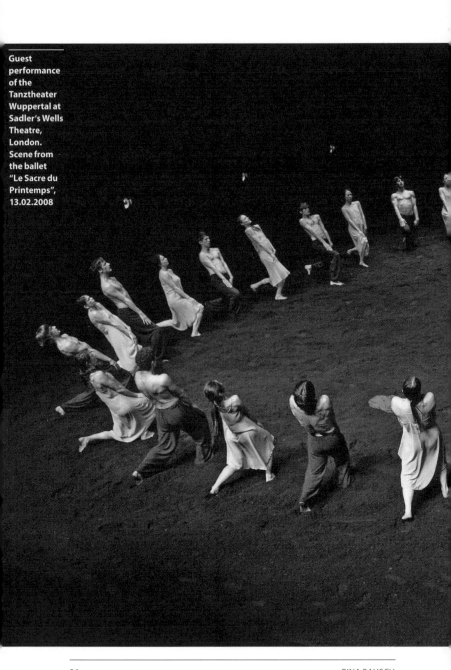

PINA BAUSCH

Jo Ann Endicott in "The Seven Deadly Sins"

# TOWARD NEW FORMS

## 'To express something that I can't express in words'
## (1974–1977)

In 1974 Pina Bausch bravely took her first steps in the direction of the new art form of dance theatre with her revue *Ich bring' Dich um die Ecke* (I'll Do You In). In an evening of dance set to music by Mahler, she had her dancers sing hit songs from the 1920s and 1930s. But it failed to connect with critics or audiences. The *WAZ* newspaper declared it a 'failure at the highest level'.[1] It was never performed again.

Bausch achieved better results with her Bertolt Brecht/ Kurt Weill evening *The Seven Deadly Sins* (1976). Here, she moved away from a pure dance form and had her dancers (together with actors and singers) sing the Brecht/Weill songs on stage. The first part of the evening was based on Bertolt Brecht's *The Seven Deadly Sins of the Petit Bourgeoisie,* which was premiered by George Balanchine in Paris in 1933 and featured Lotte Lenya.

In Bausch's version of this didactic piece about (materialistic) dreams of happiness, Jo Ann Endicott played Anna II. Her sister, Anna I, dresses and styles her so she can conform to the demands of the market. Anna II plays small-time acting roles across the country, pushed this way and that by men, measured and degraded, no more than a chattel. Bausch was not so much interested in the social conditions of the story, but concentrated instead on the conflict of the exploited woman, who has to sell her body, whilst trying to defend herself against the men's persistent advances. Bausch tells the whole story in a zippy mix of individual and revue-type group choreographies with some straightforward acting scenes, yet remains faithful to the basic plot. Rolf Borzik's design consisted of a street scene with neon lights. The orchestra was positioned at the back of the stage.

In the second part of the evening *Fürchtet Euch nicht* (Don't Be Afraid), Pina Bausch dared to take one step further towards her dance theatre. Many tropes typical of her work can be found here. The dancers sing the songs themselves. The men appear dressed as women and so play around with gender roles. The dancers address the audience directly. 'Hello, are you all there?' a woman asks at the beginning. 'We're here too!' Bausch also has the performers ironically step out of character, a feature she would continue to use.

*Fürchtet Euch nicht* consists of a loose succession of individual songs all about the hopeless search for love and happiness. As in a variety show, the dancers throw their legs about lasciviously or loll about on the floor like objects of lust. The arrangement is extremely snappy, the ensemble scenes are revue-like but do not hide the bitter sense of broken dreams. In the *Rheinischer Post*, Hartmut Regitz wrote: 'She doesn't wish to entertain us with Kurt Weill songs from *The Threepenny Opera, Kleine Groschenmusik, Happy End* or *Berlin Requiem* – instead, she points out what is going on behind it all.'[2] Actress Mechthild Großmann made her earliest appearance in *Füchtet Euch nicht*; her deep

voice and dominating yet very funny manner was to inform many of Bausch's later works. As a permanent member of the ensemble, Großmann highlighted the shift in the company from one of pure dance to one of theatre.

Pina Bausch had wanted to follow this by staging Béla Bartók's *Bluebeard*, but in the end retained only a fragment. Bausch had previously clashed with the orchestra during preparations for *The Seven Deadly Sins*; the musicians had criticized her concept and refused to put her ideas into practice. Bausch did not agree with their choice of singer for *Bluebeard*, so instead she and Rolf Borzik came up with the idea of having the music played from a mobile tape recorder that the lead character (played at the time by Jan Minarik) turned on and off himself. Because of this, the production was called *Blaubart – beim Anhören einer Tonbandaufnahme von Béla Bartóks 'Bluebeard's Castle'* ('Bluebeard – While Listening to a Taped Recording of Béla Bartók´s "Duke Bluebeard´s Castle"').

However, even before rehearsals began there were disagreements with several dancers. Many of them, as Bausch later related, had not felt happy with the previous work on the Brecht-Weill evening. 'Suddenly it was said that what I'd been doing with it was really terrible. That hit me … I didn't feel that I could do a new piece with those people. I retired to Jan Minarik's small studio along with four dancers, and we began to work … And then at some stage they all came back of their own accord, but only when they wanted to; I didn't want to have anyone who didn't want to work. It was during this piece that I started to ask questions … I only dared to do that in a small circle.'[3] The questions Bausch asked enabled her to feel her way forward, very carefully.

*Bluebeard* is a radical and disturbing piece that is not easy on the audience. Consequently there was booing at its 1977 premiere. The tape recorder, as in Beckett's *Krapp's Last Tape*, is at the centre of the white space, the floors are covered with wilted foliage. Bluebeard keeps returning to the machine, winding the music forwards and backwards, repeating the procedure again and again, testing both patience and pain barrier. The interplay between Bluebeard and Judith is reflected by the rest of the performers: the women are all versions of Judith and the men are all Bluebeard. Here Bausch takes the gruelling battle of the sexes to extremes. Bluebeard treats the women particularly brutally; he repeatedly drags them across the stage and piles them on top of each other like objects. The men and the women run at each other or up the walls, driven by longing, love, the desire for togetherness and recognition, but at the same time they humiliate and torture each other, push each other away, and yet still come crawling back for more. 'Bausch shows no mercy,' Klaus Geitel wrote in *Die Welt*, 'not to herself, not to the dancers, not to the audience. She knows how to bewitch with her art. There's not been anything like it on a German stage for a long time. Pina Bausch is carrying out an assault on all theatrical disciplines.'[4]

By her fourth season at Wuppertal Bausch had set the bar high and become a defining new force on the German dance scene. Her curiosity continued to drive her forward. She wanted to try out what was possible with an ensemble, to learn and develop herself, not necessarily out of ambition but out of a need to research. 'From the beginning I considered how I could best broach certain themes. And in doing that I found the choices opening up to me. Even today my works

Pina Bausch in conversation with Dominique Mercy during rehearsals, 1982

are created out of a formal openness. The best means of expression can be a song, a sentence or a scene – it doesn't matter. Everything is possible.'[5] She felt 'that I wanted to express something that I couldn't express in words. Something that I absolutely had to say, but not verbally. There are feelings. Or questions – I never have an answer.'[6]

Out of this came Bausch's technique of questioning, which fuelled her open way of working. Initially she would just collect material until she knew precisely the direction of a given piece. Her questioning helped her to find the right means of expression for herself. Although this might make an audience uncomfortable, the company felt that they were doing something right. As dancer Dominique Mercy said: 'We had the feeling that we were on the right path, that it was worth having the patience to carry on.'

# HAUNTING IMAGES, UNSETTLING EFFECTS

## First milestones of dance theatre (1977–1979)

In 1977, the same year as *Bluebeard*, Pina Bausch created two more pieces, *Komm tanz mit mir* and *Renate wandert aus*, both given the moniker of 'operetta' as a subtitle. Whilst *Renate wandert aus* continued to be performed until the 1980s but not since, *Komm tanz mit mir* is staged much more frequently, most recently in 2010. It is based on folk songs that are partly sung by the dancers themselves. The stage consists of white plastic sheeting that is drawn up at the back of the stage; the dancers run against it, clamber up it and use it as a slide. In the foreground large bare tree trunks lie around, used sometimes as hideaways, sometimes as weapons. As if in a nightmare, women in summer clothes are hunted and humiliated by men in thick winter coats and hats. In numerous variations, these men abuse their women, placing them round their necks like scarves, or brutally dragging them across the stage by a leg.

The action centres around a man (most recently played by Urs Kaufmann) and a woman (Jo Ann Endicott). Whilst he is lying on a deckchair dressed like a dandy in a white suit and sunglasses, she has to woo him, make herself beautiful for him, and dance for him. Her pleading verse is in vain: *Komm tanz mit mir, komm tanz mit mir, ich habe 'ne weiße Schürze für. Lass nicht ab, lass nicht ab, bis die Schürze Löcher hat* (roughly translated as: Come dance with me, come dance with me, I've a white apron 'specially. I won't give up, I won't

give up, until the apron is worn right through). Her wooing becomes ever more frantic, until she nears exhaustion. Again Bausch is dealing with a futile hunt for love and togetherness, complex power structures, and the clichéd role of a woman who enslaves herself until she unravels.

Things nearly boiled over during the premiere of Bausch's adaptation of *Macbeth* in 1978, entitled *He takes her by the hand and leads her into the castle. The others follow.* The title is taken from a Shakespearean stage direction and emphasizes the freestyle adaptation of the Bard's original. At its premiere in Bochum, members of the Shakespeare Society in the audience nearly brought the production to a halt. Apparently they had been expecting a conventional production. When the curtain rose, and virtually nothing happened for a tortuously long time – save for the dancers lying on the floor and twitching in their nightmare-plagued sleep – the onlookers grew restless. The first visitors left the theatre, and there was booing. Finally, Jo Ann Endicott plucked up her courage, stood up and yelled into the auditorium: 'If you don't want to watch this, then go home, and let us get on with our work.' After that, things settled down and the production was able to continue.

Bausch retained only fragments of *Macbeth*, and individual dialogues. Instead she used many of its motifs, such as betrayal, murder, madness, guilt and the curse of the subconscious. She mixed these with her more mundane palette of themes: recollections of childhood, the search for love and the battle between the sexes. The result was a very unusual and surreal series of images that did not follow any particular dramaturgical plot. She contrasted the comic with the tragic. There was no separation of roles. There was some dance, but not much. As in *The Seven Deadly Sins*, there was one of her so-called 'festoons', when the ensemble dance right across the stage in a row, later one of her stylistic hallmarks. Another innovation came with the use of water on stage: the dancers in *Macbeth*, driven to wash away their guilt, clean themselves with a garden hose, or use a shower and wash-basin. Though water is usually an alien presence in the theatre, it would become a common element in Bausch's work.

The same season brought *Café Müller*, performed to music by Henry Purcell; later in the 1980s the work was performed together with Stravinsky's *Rite of Spring*. It became a seminal

work for the Tanztheater and remains one of the most
performed pieces worldwide. Well into the new century,
Pina Bausch embodied the role of the somnambulant
dreamer. She wandered around in a kind of thin nightdress,
with her eyes closed and her arms outstretched, repeatedly
walking into the walls and never arriving anywhere – a rare
performance for Pina, she only allowed herself to dance in
very few productions. And yet wanting to dance was why she
started to choreograph. But later on her schedule meant that
she had no time for dancing.

Initially *Café Müller* formed part of a full evening of works
from three other choreographers: Gerhard Bohner, Gigi
Caciuleanu and Hans Pop, then assistant to Bausch. This was
the last time that other choreographers worked in Wuppertal,
Bausch's piece is the only work of the four to survive.

The set is a deserted, triste coffee house filled with
empty tables and chairs, Malou Airaudo, Meryl Tankard,
Dominique Mercy and Jan Minarik danced to melancholy
Purcell arias. Designer Rolf Borzik himself moved the chairs
away as soon as the dancers headed in one direction or
another. Later on Jean-Laurent Sasportes took over the task.
The same sequences are repeated again and again: as if in a
trance, the dancers run against the walls of the set, mostly
with their eyes closed; one dancer arranges two others into a
pair whose embrace weakens until they gradually slip away.
Love and a sense of security are not to be found here. The
work has a contextual unity and is not broken down into
scenes or musical sections. Themes of loneliness, alienation

and being lost are reflected in the piece, and Pina Bausch finds haunting images for them. The one disrupting factor in this dreamlike world is the appearance of a woman in a red wig and thick coat, who stares in consternation at these other-worldly figures.

*Arien* (1979) is a work that constitues a milestone in the Tanztheater's repertoire. It set a benchmark with its unusual set design – Rolf Borzik placed the entire stage underwater and created a kind of swimming-pool in the floor in which a hippopotamus and the dancers swim. Even though it was shortly before his death, Borzik was still providing challenging ideas that would influence the next generation of set designers, ideas that made creative use of the technical possibilities of theatre. Water would continue to play a key role in the works of Pina Bausch. Here, the dancers playfully explore its possibilities: they swim in it or float on a lilo, they spray and spit at each other, they run around splashing. The water slows down the performers' movements, clothes and hair become heavy, making the dancers appear fragile; the water also creates wonderful reflections.

The voice of Beniamino Gigli singing Italian arias lends *Arien* a generally melancholy atmosphere. The themes of grief and farewell are interrupted by some lively and boisterous passages. The dancers sit at a table as if at a wake. The hippo appears and the hostess of the party (Jo Ann Endicott) lures it over with a plate of salad. But her love for the hippo remains unrequited, as hopeless as love between people. The wake gradually falls apart, becomes wilder and more boisterous –

until the atmosphere switches. Towards the front of the stage
theatre mirrors are positioned on both sides. The dancers
dress up in front of them and make clear that this is all just
theatre. The men dress the women who are sitting in a row at
the edge of the stage, put wigs on them, wrap scarves around
them, make them up until they have faces like grotesque
dolls. The women do not resist and allow themselves to be
presented according to the men's taste.

*Keuschheitslegende* (1979) was the last play whose premiere
Rolf Borzik was able to attend. For this piece he created a sheet
of water, but this time it was simply painted onto the stage
floor. The performers loll about on all kinds of upholstered
furniture set on top it. Again animals inhabit the stage: two
archaic-looking crocodiles and a dog are brought in on leads.
The essential tone of the piece is cheerful, and there is very little
dance. The theme is clear right from the start when Mechthild
Großmann lifts up her blouse and, with a mischievous 'Take a

peek', reveals a brief glimpse of her breasts: this is an exploration of the boundaries of shame and taboos, the playful approaches and courtship rituals of men and women, sometimes delicately ironic, sometimes saucily provocative, all around ideas of love and sexuality. Rules of behaviour, which are listed, and a strict code of society etiquette, are in stark contrast to an emotional world and the longing for love and security. A dancer in a fur coat sharply orders the audience to 'smile'. Very occasionally someone disrupts the order: a woman runs shrieking around the space whilst the others try to catch her, a man suddenly appears on stage with a pistol. Such disturbing moments run through the play like a leitmotif, creating hidden depths below the superficially lively society moving around on the blue shimmering surface.

"Keuschheitslegende", 2006

# A TIMELESS AESTHETIC OF RELATIONSHIPS
## *Kontakthof*

*Kontakthof,* which premiered in 1978, has a special place in Pina Bausch's oeuvre. In 2000 a new version was produced with the subtitle 'Ladies and Gentlemen Over 65'. 'My desire, to be able to see this piece performed by ladies and gentlemen with a lot of life experience, became ever stronger with time,' Bausch later wrote. 'So I found the courage to trust *Kontakthof* to older people "over 65". People from Wuppertal. Not actors. Not dancers. Ordinary citizens of Wuppertal.'[1] Rehearsals with these senior performers were led by dancers Jo Ann Endicott, Beatrice Libonati and, subsequently, Bénédicte Billiet. Eight years after the success of this experiment, the choreographer decided the piece should be performed by young people from eleven schools in Wuppertal. Endicott and Billiet led rehearsals for *Kontakthof with Teenagers Over 14*, Bausch chose the key players and came to the final rehearsals. Both of these versions were productions in their own right, and toured as such. The last performance of the seniors' piece came in 2011, a year before the final outing for the juniors' piece in 2012.

That *Kontakthof* continues to move people decades later is proof of its timeless aesthetic. It also highlights Bausch's universal ideas about couples, relationships and community, and also how each generation can find something new in the work. Pina Bausch: '*Kontakthof* is a place to make contacts. To show yourself, to deny yourself. Along with your fears.

"Kontakthof"
with the
ensemble,
2000

Longings. Disappointments. Doubts. First experiences. First attempts. An important theme of the work is tenderness and what can come of it. Another, for example, is circus. To show something of oneself, to master oneself.'[2] Between them the three versions of the piece form a lifework for Pina Bausch that interlinks the generations. The piece is particularly suitable for lay performers because it is an ensemble piece and does not have many solo dance numbers.

The set design (from Rolf Borzik) consists of a ballroom with a high ceiling that makes the performers seem very short. Along the sides are chairs that the performers can retire to, there is a piano, and a microphone that is used to loudly trumpet private matters, feelings, thoughts and gossip, all things better kept quiet. At the start of the piece the dancers come to the front of the stage and present themselves, show their teeth and their arms, push their chests out, which probably stems from a real-life experience Pina Bausch had when auditioning at the Metropolitan Opera. This exposing of physical attributes thus reflects one aspect of a dancer's daily life.

Even when couples do come together for a few short dances, it is more of a lonely hearts' ball, accompanied by wistful hit songs from the 1920s and 1930s. The pairs provoke each other, poke each in the eye, pinch and smack each other, but always with a well-educated smile, suitable for a ball. A woman lapses into a bout of hysterical laughter and collapses, which the others pretend not to notice. Helpless attempts at attracting attention to oneself and exposing one's own sense of loneliness do not work. One woman breathes the sound 'Aua' lasciviously into a microphone, repeating it until it becomes a shout that is resentful and vulnerable. Later on this dancer interchanges it with the word 'darling' in various tones and with different emotions.

Scene from "Kontakthof" with Nazareth Panadero

In another section, the men appear to comfort one woman, but any signs of tenderness give way to intrusion: they start prodding her and stroking her, before laying into her and groping her, as she slides to the floor. Later, accompanied by wild boogie-woogie rhythms, the men sit on chairs and grab at the women without touching them, while the women press themselves against the wall, flinching and pinching themselves. A couple sitting on either side of the stage shyly undress each other in their minds, then gradually undress themselves. All attempts to come together fail. Bausch uses tragi-comic images to highlight the quest for love and togetherness, and the differences between men and women. The repetition of these motifs underscores the archetypal situations that lie somewhere between attraction and revulsion, between hope and disappointment.

These little love-games take on a particular meaning in the senior version. The childishness is in direct contrast with the advanced ages of the protagonists. One sees that the way couples behave is timeless and at the same time the performers reflect the actual experience of long-term relationships. One accepts that they know these situations well, even if they are

"Kontakthof mit Damen und Herren'ab 65'", 2008

PINA BAUSCH

artistically excessive. In the 'Over 14' incarnation, though, the teenagers' naivety and innocence in the same childish scene is consistent. With little life experience, the seemingly precocious rituals of wooing are revealed as simply hollow conventions, while their youth provides a charming contrast to the nostalgic ambience of the ballroom and the music.

The seniors' version, which was at the Tanztheater for more than ten years and toured abroad countless times, is no longer performed but it has left a deep impression and many memories remain. A documentary film by Lilo Mangelsdorff (2002) details the creation of this unusual project. Later, Anne Linsel captured the rehearsal process of the young people in 'Over 14' for a documentary film called *Tanzträume* (Dance Dreams), which premiered at the Berlinale in 2010, and has since been screened at many festivals around the world.

# THE WORKING PROCESS

## 'My work begins with questions'

*The Seven Deadly Sins* of 1976 is generally considered to be the first dance theatre piece by Pina Bausch, as it combines dancing, singing and acting. Bausch developed her working process over the next few years, refined it, and created a kind of method, an exploration of human behaviour and experience via the questions she asked her dancers during rehearsals. For her, every movement was created in the mind: 'The steps always come from somewhere else, never from the legs. Working out the movements – we do that in between times … Early on I might have started with a movement out

The choreographer's desk during rehearsals

of panic or fear and pushed the questions away. Nowadays I start with the questions.'[1]

It was during the rehearsals of *Blaubart* (1977) that Bausch first asked questions about some of the roles. In *Er nimmt sie an der Hand und führt sie in das Schloss, die anderen folgen* (He Takes Her by the Hand and Leads Her Into the Castle, The Others Follow) (1978) she developed this technique further, a necessary move as there were actors in the piece. As she explained with characteristic modesty: 'Of course I couldn't just come in with some movement phrase, but had to start elsewhere. So I asked them the questions that I was asking myself. And so this way of working really came out of necessity.'[2]

Raimund Hoghe, who was Bausch's dramaturgical collaborator between 1979 and 1990, published some rehearsal notes that shed light on the kinds of questions. For example, with *Two Cigarettes in the Dark* (1985), he wrote:

> '...First week of rehearsals, Pina Bausch starts off with questions. Asks for something 'in waltz step' and sentences 'in which God is mentioned', when does one say shit and how one can use the word mother, gives 'a little happiness' as a prompt, asks the dancers to 'do something with your stomachs' and is looking for a 'Kaspar movement'.[3]

The choreographer did not follow any concept, simply her instinct, 'because I know precisely what I am looking for,

Raimund Hoghe

but I know it from my feelings and not my head. That is why one can never ask directly. That would be too clumsy and the answer would be too banal. I know what I am looking for, but I can't explain it.[4] This made the creation of every work a time-consuming process. Jo Ann Endicott likened it to a 'birth': 'Over thirty-one years Pina gifted us nearly forty children.'

The themes also came about intuitively: 'I try to feel what I am feeling at the time, and out of this awareness I ask the dancers questions.'[6] Themes could be dreams or longings, or equally her ensemble's lack of homeland, childhood memories or fears, a dancer's concept of self, love, or the state of the world in general. Bausch: 'What are we actually doing in this world, at this time? What would be good for us? Would more laughter be appropriate? Or more sorrow? Together with my troupe I ask: how do we meet each other? How do we live together? How do we understand something?'[7]

Bausch's working process was always open, she never knew where the journey was heading: 'Our dance theatre does not provide any predetermined course, conflicts or solutions. It puts things to the test, explores processes. We enter into the feelings of others. We try to be open, we try – to put it bluntly – to feel.'[8] One can well imagine that this constant search for something unknown was not an easy process. 'As a result, I am sometimes in complete despair, because I think I am not asking the right questions. One is looking for something quite specific but does not know the path to get there.'[9] Bausch tried to look beyond the mundane, feelings, habits, memories, rituals and phrases, always starting at zero in order to develop a fresh way of seeing and to hopefully create something new.

In the early years, before any roles had to be re-cast, it was assumed that what the dancer was saying or doing on stage also related to him or her, because Bausch used the material that the dancers delivered during rehearsals. Sometimes it happened that all the dancers made movements or spoke text that had been predetermined for one person, or that the material went from one dancer to another because it suited them better.

During preparations for *Keuschheitslegende* in 1979, Raimund Hoghe noted: 'My first visit to the rehearsals. Spring. What is spring? What feelings surround it? What do you think of when you think of spring? Or a waltz. What does that mean? What does the word elicit? And chastity? What does it mean – to be chaste? And what does being unchaste look like? Pina Bausch asks. She also examines mere clichés and looks for what is behind these over-used words, the sweeping answers to a generalized life. What she does not want are familiar, fail-safe replies.'[10]

An essential part of Bausch's process is that the dancers open themselves up, bringing to light, without shame or fear, things that are also unpleasant, intimate or painful. She said:

'The dancers have to have trust, to respond with what they are feeling – above all, within the group.'[11] This is because 'the most beautiful things are usually quite hidden. So you have to take them and care for them and very slowly allow them to grow. Which requires huge mutual trust. For there are always inhibitions to overcome. That is why I like working with dancers who have a certain shyness, who do not reveal things of themselves easily. It is incredibly important that this shame, this hesitation, exists when one arrives at a certain boundary in the piece. Someone who simply produces is in the wrong place.'[12]

In Pina Bausch's work '... there is no security. I begin something and have no idea where it will take us ... there is not only fear, there is also a hope of finding something very beautiful.'[13] However the point was never to interrogate someone or expose them: 'I never ask anything private, I ask for something precise. When a dancer answers that, then that is something we all have. We know about it, but not intellectually.'[14] Bausch tried to find the universal in the particular, to filter it out, to distil and condense it, so that as many people as possible might recognize it.

Apparently, the male dancers went about answering her questions differently to their female counterparts. 'Men try out different forms to women,' said Bausch. 'They try to solve a theme with little jokes. Both men and women play little games with me. They always want to answer the question slightly differently to the way I want. They shirk the question.'[15]

In his rehearsal diary for *Two Cigarettes in the Dark* (1985), Hoghe notes that after six weeks of rehearsals Pina Bausch has asked 150 questions.[16] Only then did she start to select material from the thousands of answers, stories, images and sentences she had received, and to ask the dancers to repeat individual sequences. Then she began to arrange them. Shortly before the premiere she would cut out further individual scenes if she felt they were no longer working. Pina Bausch: 'Out of this material that has been developed I find – hopefully – trivial things which I use to carefully put something together. It is like being a painter who only has one single piece of paper and has to set about painting on it: it has to be done with a great deal of caution.'[17]

Raimund Hoghe's rehearsal notes from the programme for *1980*:

Raimund
Hoghe's
rehearsal
notes
from the
programme
for "1980"

```
Seven ways of saying 'I'm doing
great': I could fly, I could
fetch all the stars from heaven
for you, I can do everything,
I am not afraid, I could burst
with joy, I could hug everyone, I
feel so light / What is one most
afraid of: being very ill and in
terrible pain, losing someone
that I am very fond of, that I've
missed something and someone else
suffers because of it, being able
to help someone and not doing it,
noticing that I've not lived / a
reason to be sentimental: seeing an
old friend again, saying goodbye,
re-finding or being given a piece
from my childhood, seeing a film
with Marilyn Monroe, when you want
to make a phone call and no one
is there, Judy Garland's Over the
Rainbow / Things that you do to
suppress something, to not have
to think about something: watch a
film, cleaning, working, writing
something on the typewriter,
telephoning, speaking to people
about the weather and so on.
```

*Raimund Hoghe, May 1980*

# HOW THE WORKS ARE CREATED

## 'I never start at the beginning'

What actually ended up in a performance was a very small percentage of the material that was manifested during the rehearsals. 'You take five per cent, small things,' said Pina Bausch. 'Then I get the feeling that it fits like a piece of jigsaw into a puzzle that actually already exists but I don't recognize it yet.'[1] She deliberated again and again, pieced the individual scenes together in various permutations until they made sense to her. 'I never start at the beginning. I never work from the beginning to the end, but work with small little pieces that gradually get bigger, join up and expand.'[2] Her dancers appreciated her precision; as Lutz Förster said, 'the lovely

Mechthild Großmann and Lutz Förster in "1980", 2012

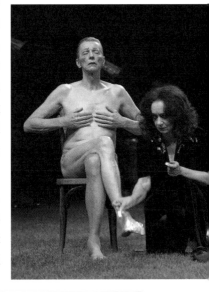

thing about Pina is that she is never satisfied, that there is always something that one can improve, make more honest.'[3] Bausch herself apparently felt this as a burden: 'I am terribly painstaking because I turn everything around and around, and make things difficult for myself. Terrible.'[4]

As if assembling a collage, Pina Bausch compiled her works elaborately and with a great sense of rhythm, timing and contrast. Solos follow ensemble scenes, quiet concentration on something specific follows hectic synchronism, and after words come dance. Repetition as a creative decision plays a key part, whether it is individual scenes being repeated during the course of an evening, such as in *Bluebeard* or *Kontatkthof*, or whether it is something like the group dance in *1980*, when the dancers march across the stage and through the auditorium. Out of the various themes, fugues and returning motifs Pina Bausch created and constructed her works like a composer. The prompt-books of her pieces (known as show-bibles), all archived by the Tanztheater, clearly display her working process. Each scene had a name which frequently only she knew. Thus during the course of rehearsals she could constantly try out new sequences and test the scenes in a new order. The music was only added right at the end.

'Overall, within the piece I always work in a contrast and compare manner,' Bausch explained. 'Hope belongs to worry, longing for the lost person belongs to loss. I would like people not to give up hope and want to embolden them.'[5] In addition, comedy alternates with tragedy in her work, and it is often humour that makes the painfully brutal scenes bearable. Emotionality was also vital to her: 'I get bored if I can't feel anything ... Cheerfulness means nothing. In each piece there is always the opposite, just as in life. That has something to do with looking for harmony.'[6] Equally, humour was essential: 'If there was nothing to laugh about, then I don't know how I could go on.'[7]

The tone of a piece – whether cheerful or sad – did not necessarily reflect Bausch's frame of mind. 'For me,' she explained, 'it is the case that personal phases of depression produce more cheerful works, and quieter periods are more likely to strengthen doubt or sorrow. It's a kind of trade-off, if you like.'[8] Which would explain why, following the death of her partner Rolf Borzik, she produced *1980 – Ein Stück von Pina Bausch*, a work that deals with mourning and farewell, but is in no way lacking humour.

In *1980* so much happens simultaneously on stage that one is only able to absorb a small part of it. That too is a hallmark of Bausch's works: they are rich in impressions and associations that would seem to be understood across the globe. And that is surely a reason to watch the performances again and again, because there is always something new to be discovered. The images she creates elude one-dimensional interpretations and are as open as the way they were devised. As Bausch said: 'I never meant: this is how it is … one can always look at them the other way around.'[9]

Nevertheless, she did feel vindicated when she sensed 'someone else feeling exactly the same way, whether one is laughing with others or feels moved, or is protecting oneself against something. Of course everyone reacts quite individually. Someone who happens to be in love sees a performance with different eyes to someone who has just experienced something terrible. But then when everything collides, it is wonderful that, on this one evening, with all these different people, we experience something together that is unique, unrepeatable.'[10] Every member of the audience can discover something for themselves, can recognize something, and be moved by something. That is precisely why the Tanztheater's pieces are unsettling – they leave the audience alone, they explain nothing. It took a few years for the audiences to learn to deal with this.

Ensemble
scene from
"1980", 2012

# PREMIERES AND REVIVALS

## 'Work in progress'

At the beginning she produced two new works per season, then at the start of the 1980s it was only one, and in 1981 due to the birth of her son, she produced none. In general, the pieces remained untitled until the premiere and were simply referred to as *Tanzabend* (an evening of dance). Matthias Schmiegelt, who was chief executive of the Tanztheater until 2001, was frequently obliged to inform the audience before the performance that they were attending a 'work in progress' and that the work was

*(From left to right): Wolfram Kremer, Heinz Theodor Jüchter, Pina Bausch, Matthias Schmiegelt (at the time chief executive of the Tanztheaters) and stage designer Peter Pabst at a press conference 1998*

not yet finished. In fact, 1991's *Tanzabend II*, a co-production with the Festival de Otoño of Madrid, remains untitled to this day. 'The premiere does not begin to show the work, but simply a station on the way to it,'[1] Bausch explained in one interview. 'A couple of times I begged for the premiere to be delayed by a week, and I always got the response: well, either you do your work punctually or you don't do it at all. To which I could only reply: fine, if those are the conditions then we will simply show what we have.'[2]

Pina Bausch would be present at nearly every performance and appear on stage at the end to take a bow with her ensemble. 'Perhaps I believe (*laughs*) that I am a talisman; I'm not too sure. Nevertheless. I do want to belong to it too … everything belongs together: the play, the ensemble, me; and so I just have to be there. The others are on the stage: I am there and watch, as always; somehow I have the feeling that it is also my performance.'[3]

Her notes on a performance came later, usually the morning after. According to her dancers they were never hurtful or personal but intended to make the work more precise, or help maintain its rhythm. 'The performances should never become routine,' she said. 'That would spell death to my work.'[4] So she would continue to polish them later, saying she was not satisfied. Sometimes the theatre pressured her to shorten a piece if it had become too long. 'That is really difficult to do. It was always like that and it continues to be so: also maintaining these works. Sometimes it is difficult to find the energy, to be overcome with joy again.'[5]

Caring for the repertoire is an integral part of the Tanztheater's work. Older works are regularly brought back into the repertoire, partly because of the many invitations to perform elsewhere, and this is often associated with long periods of re-rehearsal and cast changes. For Pina Bausch, the ideal situation was for one dancer to work on their role with their successor, but sometimes that was not possible, so video recordings came into play. There were no other recordings of the works, though. 'When someone goes away it is very difficult to replace them,' said Bausch. 'The problem is: it has not been properly recorded. No one has time for that. We have videos to keep track of things … it really only works by us all hoping that we stay together and don't forget.'[6] Initially the dancers kept written notes of their performances, as did Pina Bausch, who made a note of everything. These documents, which form part of the old show-bibles, provide full details of what the company was aiming for, as well as what props were needed.

Pina Bausch at a rehearsal for "Masurca Fogo", 1998

As head of the Tanztheater, Bausch was always present in the audience, she could sense their reactions at first hand: 'I am delighted when I see that people have understood what I wanted to talk about … but it isn't to check their judgement of the choreography, it was never ever about that. It is about humanity.'[7] She plainly tried to ignore the pressure of expectation that success brought with it via the media: 'One is constantly misunderstood. There is nothing to be done to prevent that. I have got exasperated so many times. Now I no longer get upset because I don't bother with it all. Because once you start to get involved with it you no longer have any time to work.'[8] And, for such a busy choreographer as Pina Bausch, time was the main problem.

## PRIVATE TURMOIL AND CLASSICS OF THE TANZTHEATER (1980–1986)

For Pina Bausch the year 1980 was one of private turmoil. At the beginning of that year her companion and partner, set and costume designer Rolf Borzik, died of leukaemia. He was a major influence on her work and had stamped his aesthetic mark on the Tanztheater. Bausch's response was to dive into work, and so developed *1980 – Ein Stück von Pina Bausch* (1980. A Piece by [or 'of'] Pina Bausch). It premiered that May and remains one of the most definitive of the Tanztheater's works – it was re-instated in 2012. 'I knew immediately I could not sink into sorrow,' said Bausch. 'This knowledge sustained me. It was for Rolf that I had to continue to work.'[1] She was very attached to the work. 'After Rolf's death I was so afraid that I couldn't carry on,' she said in an interview. 'It was very important for me to do this work straight away – precisely at that point, so that I had absolutely no possibility of worrying whether I might or might not be able to carry on …'[2]

In the summer of 1980, during a tour of South America, Bausch met her future partner. Ronald Kay was a German-Chilean professor who taught Aesthetics and Literature at the Universidad de Chile. He moved to Wuppertal and lived with Bausch right up until her death. She soon became pregnant and in September 1981, at the age of forty-one, she gave birth to a son, Rolf Salomon, who today heads the Pina Bausch Foundation in Wuppertal.

'After I went through the experience of how a person dies, I was also able to experience how a person is born. And how this affects one's view of the world. How a child experiences things. How it views everything without preconception. How it places such natural trust in one. Just to comprehend that a person is born. Without mentioning the experience of how and what is happening to one's own body, how it changes. It all happened without me having to do anything. And how all of this flows back into my pieces and my work.'[3]

Pina Bausch's already tight schedule became tighter still. In 1981 and 1983 the choreographer produced no new works. Moreover, in 1983 she took over the running of the dance department of the Folkwang-Hochschule in Essen from Professor Hans Züllig. She took this responsibility very seriously, and as well as teaching in Essen, invited both her classes to Wuppertal once a week. 'I don't only want to be a manager who signs things,' she said. 'I wanted to get to know the students and work with them, make something with them.'[4]

Hans Züllig
(1914-1992)

She ran the dance department in Essen for ten years. In 1993 she handed this task over to one of her former dancers, Lutz Förster. A close collaboration grew out of this cooperation with the Folkwangschule that proved mutually beneficial: whenever needed, the Tanztheater was able to engage young dancers for individual performances or tours of *The Rite of Spring*. At the same time, promising dancers gained their first professional experience at the Tanztheater.

Despite the demands of motherhood and teaching, Pina Bausch continued to be extraordinarily creative and productive. The works that were created during the first half of the 1980s were some of the Tanztheater's most distinctive. *Nelken* (1982) is the one that is performed most often worldwide, while *1980* and *Auf dem Gebirge hat man ein Geschrei gehört* (On the Mountain A Cry Was Heard) are regarded as quintessential examples of the art form that is dance theatre.

*1980 – Ein Stück von Pina Bausch,* combines and repeats solo and group scenes, silence and sound, easy-listening and electronic music, performed scenes and dance scenes (although the latter are few in number) into one *Gesamtkunstwerk* of dance theatre. Old English arias

"1980" was last re-rehearsed in 2012

are juxtaposed with songs by the Comedian Harmonists and Judy Garland's 'Somewhere over the Rainbow'. Peter Pabst contributed his first set design for a Pina Bausch piece: a meadow on which a single (stuffed) deer stands. The production explored a range of themes dealing with lost childhood. One dancer spoons soup out of a huge bowl, 'one spoon for mama, one spoon for papa', until he has gone through the entire group. One female dancer places a colleague across her knees, and rocks him to Brahms's song 'Guten Abend, gute Nacht' and playfully smacks his naked bottom. Atop a polar bear skin, Lutz Förster sprawls on his stomach like a baby. In the absence of guests for her birthday, a young woman repeatedly wishes herself 'happy birthday' and blows out a lighter.

Also reflected in *1980* are themes of sorrow and farewell. The ensemble, dressed in evening dress, say goodbye to their hosts politely in an ever-changing vocabulary. There is an announcement in different languages that points to the departure of a ship. The dancers form tight-standing groups at the edge of the stage, wipe the tears from their cheeks and clap their hands gently; a small dance of gestures develops out of this repetitive sequence. The dancers also come together in pairs or dance their way through the auditorium in a trademark line. At the back of the stage, one woman dances a playful solo under a water sprinkler.

In the second part of the evening the dancers vie with one another in a kind of perplexing exhibitionism. They ask: who has what scars and illnesses? They lie down in the meadow as if they are sunbathing and each reveals only one part of their body. Dancers characterize the land of their birth in just three words: an American says, 'John Wayne, hamburger, Cadillac,' while a Pole says, 'Chopin, vodka, Nijinksy'. Meanwhile, an old magician makes things disappear, and a geriatric acrobat practises at the barre. Youth and old age, memory and transience, arrivals and departures, melancholy and absurd comedy – all of these come together to create a complex collage of dance theatre that lasts some three and a half hours.

Another work produced later in 1980 was *Bandoneon*. A bandoneon is an instrument not dissimilar to an accordion that is used for tango music in Argentina. Pina Bausch had heard this music on the tour of South America and took

Scene from
"Bandoneon"

it as inspiration for this melancholy piece on her return. *Bandoneon* takes place in a sort of bar room filled with tables and chairs that are then mostly removed before the interval, leaving behind a bare room (for more, see the chapter entitled 'The Set Designers'). Old black and white photos hang on the walls, mainly of boxers, although there is also one of Pina Bausch's parents in Solingen. Even though the piece is threaded with melancholy tango music, no classical tango is ever danced. Sometimes the women sit frontways on the men's shoulders and move in time to the music, while at other times couples dance on their knees, or the men and women cradle each other on the floor, locked tightly together. The steps are frequently slowed down, the scenes stretch out and become a test of patience. Bausch is examining the rituals of couples dancing together and looking for new forms of unity.

What does dance mean, and what does the audience expect of it? Bausch uses a myriad of ideas to illuminate the dancing and the need for the performers to produce something of themselves. One dancer pulls a tutu over his head and, embarrassed, does a few exercises, because that is what is expected of him. A female dancer dresses up another dancer and forces her to smile before brutally pushing her head into a bucket of water. Another dancer tells of a teacher who held a burning cigarette under his legs so that he would keep them high off the ground. Personal experiences of the dancers are reflected in physically exaggerated moves. Legs are bent and twisted in order to question the ethics of dancing drills. Bausch subverts audience expectations by halting the action in the middle of the piece, and letting silence reign. 'Do something!' a dancer calls out from the stage, turning the tables on the audience.

The next works, *Walzer* and *Nelken*, both premiered in 1982, the last year that saw two premieres from the Tanztheater. After that, the rhythm of the company changed to one premiere a year, usually in the spring.

Domnique Mercy in "Bandoneon"

Alongside several ensemble dances, it is the spoken scenes that dominate *Walzer*; the music plays a secondary role. The themes of *Walzer,* which is performed on a stage filled with floral arrangements, include family ties, departures and arrivals, self-presentation, the creative process of the Tanztheater. Each of the dancers present items they treasure that belonged to a relative, or list their nicknames. Jan Minarik's appearances are like a running gag throughout the piece: he talks into the microphone about the questions Bausch asked during the rehearsals and how he replied. 'And then I am to do something with a white handkerchief,' he says and waves it in the air. Another dancer relates how Pina asked him what one would think if one was sitting in a trap like an animal. Every dancer contributes a response, sometimes a personal one, sometimes an amusing one, sometimes just a banality, ironically revealing just how the choreographer collects her material. Unusually, *Walzer* was created as a co-production with the Holland Festival and premiered in 1982 in Amsterdam. Only later did it open in Wuppertal, before it went out on tour. It was revived in 1987, but after that was never performed again.

When *Nelken* (Carnations) premiered at the Wuppertal Opera House in 1982, it ran for nearly four hours. Bausch was not happy and shortened it to a version about one hundred minutes long, which was performed in May 1983. Apparently, a field of carnations she saw in Chile during the South American tour of *1980* inspired her to create a set full of paper carnations that acts as a dream landscape. The piece, from this first heyday of the Tanztheater, is dense and captivating, and consequently is frequently revived.

The audience leaves the theatre with Sophie Tucker's wistful 'The Man I Love' running through their minds as it runs as a leitmotif through the piece. On two occasions,

Lutz Förster signs to the song, turning the movements into a kind of arm-dance that vividly illustrates a longing for love and security. Julie-Ann Stanzak stalks through the carnation field, her legs bare, an accordion clutched to her chest, describing the four seasons through gestures. Finally, the ensemble members form one line and walk in a circle making those same gestures to describe the eternal cycle of life.

A man repeatedly accosts the others with a microphone in his hand to acoustically amplify their pulse rate, polices individual dancers – all foreigners – he asks them for their papers, and sets them humiliating tasks, such as 'imitate a dog on all fours'. Also featuring in this threatening scenario are men with German Shepherd dogs who patrol the field of carnations. High metal towers that look like border control posts turn out to be diving platforms for four stuntmen, who fall onto a pile of empty boxes. Appearance and reality all play a role in an apparent fist fight between four men all wishing to impress a woman.

Julie Anne Stanzak and Lutz Förster in "Nelken", 2008

Scene from "Nelken" with Dominque Mercy, Andrey Berezin, Michael Strecker und Lutz Förster *(from left to right)*, 2008

Providing a contrast to these hard types are male dancers in women's clothing. Again and again they brave a little dance in their female costumes and consequently drive the women off their exposed position on a table. The women then have to continue dancing under the table. The suppression follows without words. The men clearly are at the heart of *Nelken*. They can only reveal themselves as vulnerable and emotional when they are together. 'If there's a dispute in the air and things are looking bad, then I act all sensitive', says one, whilst dancing ring-a-roses with his two colleagues.

The role of a dancer in dance theatre is shown in a variety of different ways. 'I haven't done it for a long time, but you did want to see it', says one performer, and leaps into the air. Dominique Mercy performs turns, grand jetés and pirouettes and shouts aggressively to the audience, playing with their expectations: 'You want to see ballet?', 'What else do you want?' and 'I told you I can do it.' This scene could be seen as an icy response to Bausch's critics, who would prefer to watch classical ballet as opposed to dance theatre. Later on the ensemble open up to the audience, revealing why they became dancers in the first place: one was in love with a dancer, one said 'by chance', another replied, 'I wanted to be different to the others'.

*Auf dem Gebirge hat man ein Geschrei gehört* (On the Mountain a Cry was Heard) had its premiere in 1984. It was inspired by a quote from the Bible (Matthew 2,18) which refers to Herod's slaughter of the innocents; the music in the piece comes comes from Heinrich Schütz's *St Matthew Passion.* As in *The Rite of Spring,* earth covers the stage which the dancers stalk across. Sometimes they lie on the ground and seemingly 'swim' on the uneven surface. Bausch makes full use of repetition; there is scarcely a scene that is seen only once. The atmosphere is eerie and threatening, not only when the stage is engulfed by a fog so the performers appear to get lost. The many short scenes symbolically lay bare dark desires and fears.

Michael Strecker and Nazareth Panadero in "Auf dem Gebirge hat man ein Geschrei gehört", 2008

Jan Minarik (later on, Michael Strecker) plays a nightmarish figure dressed throughout in swimming trunks, a bathing cap and rubber gloves, his face distorted by a rubber band across his nose. He brings balloons to blow up and burst, takes a woman and uses her to hit a man, and pulls another woman along by her hair. With a red pen he draws lines on

a woman who repeatedly throws herself in front of him and exposes her back as if he is whipping her. As is frequently the case in Bausch's work, the men and women don't come together unless under duress. In one scene, repeated several times, a group of men catch hold of a man and woman and force them to kiss. Some individuals are able to get away from the group and dance by themselves, lost, with only an outstretched arm – that seems remote-controlled – to direct them where to go.

Youth and old age, blooming and fading, are the leitmotifs running through the piece. One man paints grey onto Beatrice Libonati's hair as she stands at the footlights and looks sadly out into the auditorium. She sucks in her lips and turns into an old woman. Later on, in her loneliness, she wails at a paper moon or hides between the trees that sway at the end of the stage sky and desolately calls out 'Hello'. There

"Two Cigarettes in the Dark", 2011

PINA BAUSCH

is no sympathy, and emotions and tears are contrived, such as when the men push their faces into freshly-cut onions. At the end, an orchestra consisting of OAPs make an impressive entrance.

*Two Cigarettes in the Dark*, which premiered in 1985, features only eleven dancers, and as a result, the work has frequent quiet sections with little action and no music. It seems reduced and dark, and there are seldom any comic moments. What music there is comes from the classical works of Monteverdi, Beethoven and Purcell, as well as *minnelieder*, but they are usually extracts, rarely played in full.

The set is a tall, white room with shop windows on three sides, and with different vegetation behind the glass: a desert with cactuses, a luscious green jungle, and an aquarium with fish which a dancer climbs into and dives under for a short while. A couple flee into the jungle as if into paradise but they are shot down by a pistol-toting woman. 'Come in, my husband is at war,' says Mechthild Groβmann at the beginning of the piece, which sets the fatalistic tone. It is a rather sad group that has gathered for the party. The men and women stay mainly separate. If they do come together then it is very much everyone for themselves, like the couple sitting on a chair panting away – the act of love as a mechanical ritual during which one still remains alone.

A man calls for an imaginary barnyard fowl, axe and chopping block at the ready. Everyone really wants to run away, perhaps into the imaginary worlds suggested by the shop windows? Possible means of escape are tried out: a woman attempts to fly away on a carpet; men and women in pairs shuffle along the floor towards the door but can't clamber up the steps; one man wades across the desert in diving flippers; other dancers slip with their feet wrapped as if on ice, yet all remain trapped in this world.

PINA BAUSCH

# WUPPERTAL ON THE ROAD

## 'Refuelling with passion and curiosity'

Towards the end of the 1970s Pina Bausch and her Tanztheater started touring internationally. An increasing number of invitations for guest appearances meant that the reputation of this unusual company grew on nearly all continents, with the exception of Africa. In 1987, the Tanztheater even guested in the former East Germany and in autumn 2009 the ensemble visited an Arabic country for the first time, namely Egypt. But the majority of the guest performances took place in Paris, followed by Italy, New York and Tokyo. The most frequently performed works were *The Rite of Spring* and *Café Müller* with around forty tours each, followed by *Nelken, Kontakthof* and 1998's *Masurca Fogo*.

These numerous invitations also ensured that many works remained in the repertoire. The Tanztheater could not have presented so many productions before sold-out audiences in Wuppertal alone. Besides, the Tanztheater shared the Wuppertal performance spaces – an opera house and a theatre – with the opera and performance departments of the Wuppertal stages. Since the theatre closed, everything is now concentrated in the opera house. Without these tours the Tanztheater could never have funded so many performances, they are a substantial part of how the company is financed. The ensemble spends several months a year abroad and thus covers part of their costs. 'The touring

*Opposite:*
Setting off
on the South
American
tour, 1980

becomes ever more important year on year,' explains Dirk Hesse, the Tanztheater's chief executive since 2011. 'We do thirty performances a year in Wuppertal, which is a good starting point. We have to do fifty-five to sixty performances abroad in order to be able to balance the books at the end of the year. The constant demand for guest performances is absolutely essential.'

The touring became an integral part of the life of the company and in turn, generated material for an ever increasing number of new works. Pina Bausch: 'Sometimes one has just got to look through a window.'[1] In 1986 *Viktor* became the first collaboration with an international partner (a so-called residency piece), in this case Teatro Argentina and the city of Rome. After that the number of co-productions, and thus tours, increased. Bausch would travel to the region in question with her dancers for research purposes and to gain inspiration. 'Wonderful, exhilarating travels,'[2] she called them. 'Love stories' happened both in and with a new city. Although Bausch didn't really enjoy flying, she tolerated it in order to get to know new countries, people and cultures: 'It is an incredible piece of luck to be somewhere and not simply be a tourist, but to work there, to come into contact with other people.'[3] Her passion and curiosity were constantly refuelled. She studied people and their customs, always wanting to know more, and as she emphasized, was extremely grateful to be able to have these experiences: 'I was able to experience so much and would like to communicate even more of it.'[4]

'I don't know if homesickness is perhaps the same as *wanderlust*. Sometimes I think it is the same thing. I am happy to come back, equally I like to go away.'[5] And she also admitted: 'If we didn't go on our travels, then I would no longer be in Wuppertal. I would not have been able to muster up this energy here.'[6] As a 'Solingerin', she had been connected to Wuppertal since childhood. Nonetheless, she never dreamt she would spend her entire life there. She frequently stressed that her work was not bound to a particular place. She was offered positions by many artistic directors, notably Peter Zadek in 1985 (the Schauspielhaus in Hamburg) and, before that, Arno Wüstenhöfer made her an offer when he moved to Bremen in 1977. But no offer could compete with the facilities she had at Wuppertal. By 1979 she had her own rehearsal stage in the shape of the Lichtburg,

Rehearsal space in the Lichtburg in Barmen, which was a cinema in the sixties

a former cinema, which was situated very close to the opera house. Here she could rehearse at any time, independent of stage re-builds and the mandatory rest periods for the technical staff. In 1997, the Tanztheater was also given administrative offices outside the opera house. Two years later, the Tanztheater became a GmbH (a limited liability company) and was thus independent of the Wuppertal stages; since Pina Bausch's death, the City of Wuppertal has become the sole shareholder. The state of North-Rhine Westphalia provides an annual subsidy of about one million Euros.

Pina Bausch would only ever have considered moving to another theatre if she could have taken all her dancers with her. But they too felt at ease in the region, and the tours were a kind of compensation for the constraints of Wuppertal. 'Some suffer very much from living here,' said Bausch. 'It is difficult for people who come from countries where the sun is always shining. They long for colour, for sun, for warmth. But then there are others who find travelling around simply too much. They would much prefer to stay and work here and travel less.'[7] At one point, when a move to Paris was on the cards, she explained in an interview: 'We discussed it with the company and I thought, they're all bound to want to go, there's so much rain here and it's grey and joyless. But everyone wanted to stay in Wuppertal.'[8]

Pina Bausch could equally have worked well elsewhere. Nevertheless, she appreciated Wuppertal, a perfectly ordinary town. In very close proximity to her rehearsal rooms at the Lichtburg cinema in Barmen are a peepshow, a fast-food

restaurant and a bus-stop, offering a choreographer more than sufficient opportunity to observe: 'The people who stand there always look so sad and tired. It is important for me to see what kind of world we live in, important to me and my work.'[9] Another argument for Bausch to stay in Wuppertal was that 'more often than not, the so-called arts are created in the smaller theatres, and the larger houses buy them off the smaller ones.'[10]

As she agreed to the touring committments far in advance, Pina Bausch remained in Wuppertal and lived all those years in the same apartment on Fingscheid in Unterbarmen, which is where the Foundation is situated today. 'I can't even move out of my apartment,' she once said. 'I would love to have something nicer and larger. I don't get round to doing anything. All my energy and time goes into my work.'[11]

# THE ERA OF CO-PRODUCTIONS

## Translating the influences of a country into dance
## (1986–1999)

The great period of co-productions began in 1986 with
*Viktor*, and right up until Bausch's last work, which was
created in co-operation with Chile, co-productions shaped
the work of the Tanztheater. The influences from a country
– whether these were music, customs, traditions, intellectual
influences, rituals or everyday life – were all, in Pina Bausch's
words, 'translated into dance'.[1] Getting to know the foreign
and then sharing it with others became an important driver
for the choreographer's work, and it turned her dance theatre
into a universal global theatre understood by all. Moreover,
alien influences and sources of inspiration ensured that the
Tanztheater constantly re-invented itself, never got stuck, but
remained fresh and alive as it absorbed new challenges and
influences. The content of its productions changed in line

Banner for
the first dance
festival at the
Schauspielhaus
Wuppertal 1998

with the impressions and moods that Pina Bausch brought back from abroad and then digested.

Works were created with the help of Brazil, Los Angeles, India, Korea, Japan, Vienna, Madrid, Hong Kong, Lisbon, Budapest, Istanbul and Chile; relationships with the cities of Rome and Palermo meant that Italy was a frequent co-operation partner. 'It's almost as if we are married now,'[2] Bausch once said. The local Goethe-Instituts around the world were frequently involved. The Tanztheater expanded its network with different theatres worldwide. Because of the friendships forged during these co-productions, top companies from all over the world travelled to the dance festivals organized by Bausch. Four of these in all were held in Wuppertal and North-Rhine Westphalia: the Tanzfest in 1998 and 2001, and the Internationales Tanzfest NRW in 2004 and 2008.

To illustrate the nature of these co-operations, Bausch described how she once bought a buffalo bone from a Native American in the United States. 'The bone had many tiny symbols written on it. I then discovered that all the people who had bought a part of the buffalo, like me, had written their address in a book. And so the buffalo had spread itself everywhere. Together we are part of a network, like this buffalo, distributed across the world.'[3]

The visibility of the cultural influences varied according to the co-producing country. Some works, such as *Palermo Palermo,* incorporates a great deal from the partner city; while others, such as *Como el musguito en la piedra, ay si, si, si …* make scant reference to the co-producing partner, in this case Chile. Pina Bausch never directly transposed references in the documentary sense; they were always poetically estranged, encrypted, aesthetically heightened and artistically condensed on stage. Folklore was rarely present, unless it was in an ironic form, such as the man in a South American knitted poncho and woolly hat in the Chilean piece.

The first co-production, *Viktor* (1986), was created in collaboration with the Teatro Argentino and the City of Rome, but the piece only references the co-producing partner in small details. The women's dresses in muted colours and the fur coats recall Italian films from the 1940s and 1950s. The music of this dense piece ranges from Tchaikovsky to traditional folk music from the different regions of Italy.

The stage resembles a catacomb, a deep grave with earth walls that a grave-digger is slowly filling in. The ladders suggest an archaeological dig. Although this dark piece does contain some comic scenes, Bausch is constantly circling the subject of death. Right at the start a couple lie lifeless on the floor and are married by a man, who takes their heads and makes them nod and kiss. Later on a man is laid out as if in a morgue and is covered with a sheet – one of the more comic moments occurs when he is woken by an alarm clock and demands a coffee. Another man pants into a microphone as if to convince himself that he is alive. One dancer in a black cowl, who leads a procession of women but keeps getting the rows mixed up, resembles death himself.

One scene is reminiscent of Rome and its fountains: two men use a woman as a water fountain by filling her mouth with water. They then wash themselves under the stream of water she spits out – an unusual kind of exploitation. Another scene tends towards the comic: a man is sitting in a restaurant and is prevented from ordering anything by a bored waitress with a cigarette in her mouth. Couples dance in a tight embrace, or as if in a musical revue, to 'Puttin' on the Ritz.' Silvia Kasselheim stuffs veal into her pointe shoes and dances *en pointe* before finally leaving the stage, irritated. Pina Bausch uses the inspiration from abroad and condenses it into a new whole, along with her own themes of the battle between the sexes, fears about the state of the world, and the

Nazareth Panadero in a scene from "Viktor", 2007

self-image of dancers. The unfamiliar is reflected in the familiar and this fresh approach makes the familiar seem foreign.

Although *Ahnen* (1987) was not created in co-production with another country, its set of huge cacti, similar to those found in Arizona, suggests thoughts of travel. The exotic scenery offers a background to all kinds of outlandish figures. Comical and poetically-delicate scenes interchange with subliminally-threatening and provocative ones. A man and woman dance, wound tightly around each other, then her dress catches fire at the hem. One man shaves another whose hands are tied and whose protests at having an orange in his mouth are ignored. Bausch exaggerates the banalities of everyday life and pillories the decadent and superfluous – such as when a servant irons his (armed) mistress's newspaper,

PINA BAUSCH

or when men dab away at a woman with bread, or when a despairing woman, lying on the floor, calls for room service.

*Ahnen* is dominated by contrasts: silence is broken by the sound of a jackhammer, melancholy songs give way to booming punk music that turns the atmosphere aggressive. Three men lie on beds, as if in a sanatorium. Dominique Mercy has stuck eyes onto his closed eye-lids and dreamily sings a love aria, whilst lying next to him a stereotypical Frenchman explains the words to a stereotypical Chinese man. The desire to succumb to rest is made clear when a man makes himself a bed out of hay, or a woman lies down to sleep amongst the cacti whilst another builds a protective wall around her. Meanwhile, a walrus waddles through the cacti, looking completely out of place. A sad Native American fully kitted out in feathers seems to have fallen through a time loop.

In 1988 Pina Bausch worked on a brand-new project, the film *Die Klage der Kaiserin* (The Complaint of an Empress), which opened in cinemas the following year. For the first time, she translated her themes into images for the big screen, filmed outdoors around Wuppertal. It would remain the sole film project she directed, although she appeared as a performer in Federico Fellini's 1983 film *E la nave va* (And the Ship Sails On) as the blind Duchess.

Bausch's co-productions continued with *Palermo Palermo*, with the city's Teatro Biondo as partner. At the start, the entire proscenium arch is virtually filled in by a wall. It soon tips over and crashes down, leaving a dusty field of rubble which acts as terrain for the dancers. As this piece was created in

1989, the same year the Berlin Wall fell, many people thought that Bausch was referring to that historical event, but she disputed that many times. The fall of the Wall enabled her to look behind the façades at the rubble of society, in which there are no commonalities, and where every individual has to fight to survive.

Sometimes an oppressive silence reigns, but then the music – frequently world music, African songs or drumming – plays on what feels like an endless loop. Church bells and chirping cicadas create a southern atmosphere that is then abruptly replaced by silence and a change in lighting. Julie Shanahan opens the sequence of images with a dance. Then she tells the men what they have to do: 'Take my hand, hug me.' But it's never quite right for her, so she walks off, frustrated. These scenes repeat themselves. Later on she talks of a suicidal person who was prompted to jump by a group of onlookers. She herself appears with a stocking mask and a pistol as a threatening lone fighter – armed and prepared for anything.

Dancers step on the fallen wall. A woman puts sugar on her lips and demands: 'Kiss me.' Yet her advances are in vain. Men carry women around like dolls. One man attempts to impress a woman by running behind her like a monkey with his arms hanging down.

This fight for survival produces strange effects, as when one woman wants to have her spaghetti all to herself: 'It's all mine.' Even the animals are scrabbling around for food: one man spreads some scraps of food out on an old newspaper,

a dog comes in and eats it up greedily. A dancer tells of a dog that laid down alone in a dustbin to die. Italy's problems with rubbish are reflected ironically in a dance where the dancers step in formation across the stage and liberally and rhythmically distribute the rubbish. Later on the dancers form a kind of protest movement and throw stones at the rear wall of the stage. Loneliness, rage, sorrow, alienation and poverty are the themes of *Palermo Palermo*. As soon as a lighter atmosphere threatens to break through, blossoming cherry trees swing down from the stage heavens and the play ends. The performers frequently come together for group dances, before individual actions or solo dances begin to dominate, mainly performed at the footlights in front of the pieces of wall. There is a lot more dancing in *Palermo Palermo* than in *Viktor*, and it heralded a new phase of Pina Bausch's work, in which dance, and above all solo dances, began to proliferate.

"Palermo Palermo"

"Palermo
Palermo"

*Tanzabend II*, a co-production with the Festival de Otoño in Madrid, which had its premiere in 1991, remains the only Bausch work without a title. It was performed just a few times and after 1993 disappeared from the Tanztheater's repertoire altogether. Similarly, *Das Stück mit dem Schiff* (The Piece with the Ship), which was created in 1993 without a co-producing partner; after going on several tours it remained on the programme until 1996, but has not been revived since. Neither, so far, has *Ein Trauerspiel*, which was originally unveiled in 1994 as a co-production with the Wiener Festwochen.

In contrast, *Danzón* (1995) has remained a constant in the Tanztheater repertoire, possibly because it has a small cast of just thirteen dancers. Apart from *Café Müller*, it remains the only choreography in which Pina Bausch herself danced. In this piece, which is dominated by projections, the choreographer, in black trousers and pullover, stands in front of a picture of fish in an aquarium and performs a very introverted dance, using her arms only – they stretch out longingly in all directions without her legs ever moving from

*Opposite:* Pina
Bausch in
"Danzón"

the spot. This static dance lies at the heart of the production, and the swaying arms are reminiscent of a wave, as if Bausch wanted to say goodbye. After her death, Aleš Čuček (a male dancer) took over the role, a lovely disassociation, as the dancer could not be seen as attempting to replace Pina Bausch.

The stage for *Danzón* is empty. Images and films are projected onto a gauze that transform the stage into a blooming cherry orchard, a mountain landscape, or a seascape. Travel and longing for the unknown are reflected in the piece. A woman in walking boots and a thick coat walks on stage and begins to dance. Another woman, thickly-padded, also attempts a delicate little dance with her feet but she is restricted by her voluptuous body shape. Dancers lie in small tents and tell each other stories in atmospheric fading light. A quiet *fado*, or Japanese music, runs through the scenes, in which one action dissolves into another and all the dancers are rarely on stage simultaneously. A man dressed like a giant baby in a nappy crawls across the stage as if in a nightmare. He weighs down two women with stones, while they write on the floor as if dreaming. Later on he drags one of the women across the stage after him as if she were a doll. Another man with cardboard rabbit ears waves like a lonely alien into the audience. An exotically-dressed woman dances with a rubber snake.

Wearing only a feather boa, Mechthild Großmann, the actor of the ensemble, copies dance moves and brags about the advantages of her pink feather knickers. Such absurd, comic scenes are juxtaposed with quieter dances frequently tinged with melancholy. The title *Danzón* (which in Spanish means dance-rage) sums up many of the solos. Disturbing scenes break up the ostensible merriment. A woman dances a solo on the floor whilst another shovels earth over her. A couple sit on a see-saw and tease each other. The see-saw, however, consists of nothing more than an iron bar – and without seats, it is closer to torment than fun. As with much of Bausch's work, there is ambivalence rather than concrete classification.

*Nur Du* (Only You), which premiered in 1996, was the Tanztheater's sole co-production with North America, specifically the universities of Los Angeles, Arizona State, Berkeley and Austin. It contains an unusual number of references to American idiosyncrasies and clichés. Julie Shanahan as a blonde Hollywood diva sprawls on a 'sofa' consisting of men's backs. Helena Pikon enters as a showgirl wearing suspenders, squeals an exaggerated 'Welcome', and jumps into the air. American dancer Julie Anne Stanzak, as a leaping cheerleader, encourages an imaginary sports team. Two dancers show how one can imaginatively recycle packing materials by wearing bikini tops made of paper cups.

The stage consists of tree trunks from mammoth trees whose tops are too high to be seen. They epitomize a yearning for nature in an artificial society, but their size also feels menacing. A dancer in a blue evening dress talks about the weather and presents the art of small talk. There is jazz and South American music, but also the flute music of America's original inhabitants. Many scenes with particularly striking costumes interchange with dance scenes. The longing for closeness remains mainly one-sided: a man tosses the hair of a woman into his face, another man lets a woman suck his thumb. A woman lets herself fall forward and is only caught by a man just before she hits the floor. A man forms a woman in accordance with his wishes: he puts a blonde wig on her head and shoves balloons down her t-shirt to act as breasts.

Others show what they can do to impress. One woman practises on a horizontal bar, another slides into the splits and splendidly rolls her R's. A careful approaches to the precious resource of water dominates: a man bathes in a polythene sheet that is held up by others. Another man washes his feet in a bucket. A third man wears goggles, but also has a transparent plastic bag around his head that he is filling up with water from above. These are playful flights into another

"Nur Du"

PINA BAUSCH

world, but they also express a kind of terrible masochism. Yet despite such disturbed scenes, *Nur Du* remains a mainly cheerful piece and ushered in a more conciliatory, joyful phase in Pina Bausch's work. It introduced several new, strong personalities who perform highly energetic solo dances: Rainer Behr, Eddie Martinez and Fernando Suels Mendoza were to become defining figures of the Tanztheater over the next few years.

*Der Fensterputzer* (The Window Cleaner) was a co-production with the Hong Kong Arts Festival and premiered in February 1997, five months before Hong Kong was returned to China. The previous year Pina Bausch and her ensemble had travelled to the territory and brought back many impressions which she worked into the new production. The stage is black, apart from a large hill of red blossoms, bauhinia flowers from the new Hong Kong coat of arms. Projections show street gullies with many illuminated adverts, dancers ride around on bicycles. One dancer sings a Chinese song into the microphone whilst three women sit and smoke under her skirt, which she is holding aloft. The window cleaner of the title is swaying on a seat along a superimposed high-rise building façade which slowly rises. The red blossoms rain down from a black stage sky, are hurled into the air by the crack of a firework, or

Andrey Berezin in "Der Fensterputzer"

arranged on the floor. Poetic images infuse this lively and atmospheric work.

Even the scenes between men and women are conciliatory and friendly. 'Do you have a wish?' ask two men as they carry a woman, her desire for chocolate immediately satisfied. A man and a woman dream of sharing a watermelon and sing a little song about it. Even the men, who are using a woman as a battering ram against a pile of boxes, don't seem to mean any harm. A man fans a woman, while another holds out her dress so that she can slide into it as she runs past. A couple are embroiled in a power struggle over the placement of an occasional table. Mechthild Großmann causes great merriment by describing in detail her husband's bad breath, which does not prevent her from wanting to kiss him.

This carefree atmosphere is reflected in countless dances. Frequently one solo goes straight into another, or several dancers dance in a line, each one lost in their own movements. When several solo dancers share one piece of music, the dancers express themselves in strikingly different ways: self-absorbed, or extrovert, or with a delicate movement of arms and legs, or sharp, or tormented, or sometimes spinning on the floor like a break-dancer. Pina Bausch gives them room to reveal their individuality. One man repeatedly throws himself on the ground towards the women standing around him, thus scaring them out of their (dance) territory. The image from this piece that truly lingers is in the last scene: as if on an outing, the men and women wander across the hill

of flowers, whilst the background projections show changing landscapes.

"Der Fensterputzer"

*Masurca Fogo* was created as a co-production with Expo 1998 Lisbon and the Goethe-Institut based there. The stage consists of a white room into which a stream of lava has poured, and is now solidified. It narrows the performance space at the front and acts as a dark contrast to the colourful projections showing the Cape Verde Islands. There are people dancing and making music as well as blooming landscapes, the sea, and brightly-coloured flamingos. The evening begins with a solo performance that celebrates the *joie de vivre* of dance. Twice, a line of couples dances across the stage. In a particularly exuberant scene, the dancers build a provisional bar with a few planks of wood and happily party away inside it. Despite the poverty, the image suggests that dancing together brings joy.

Thematically, Pina Bausch gradually brings the difficulties between the sexes centre stage. Men and women simply cannot get together, despite many attempts. Julie Shanahan

applies cream to the bare knees of Rainer Behr, who is wearing swimming trunks; however, as he wants to thank her with a kiss, he is far too short for her – and someone else has to lift him up. A dancer says to a woman, 'I like you, I want to kiss you,' but when the chosen woman comes over to him he walks off. Similarly, when a woman holds her hand out for a man to kiss, she pulls it away before he lifts it to his lips. A couple dance wrapped tightly around each other, but their gaze is fixed on a television. A man slaps a woman on her behind; she takes her revenge by secretly dunking his tie in his drink. In comparison with Pina Bausch's earlier attacks, these scenes come across as mild and almost conciliatory. What remains ambivalent is the groaning of a woman into a microphone that continues throughout the play – on the one hand passionate, on the other hand, full of pain; it could be an expression of joy or sorrow, depending on one's perspective.

Even when the woman is caught up by the men and carried around, she remains isolated from them.

In *O Dido* (1999), Bausch again played a variation on her themes of *joie de vivre* and passion. A black stone dominates the back of the stage, lying there like a stranded meteorite. Again projections of plants dominate the piece. Dancers disappear into the colourful images, almost becoming one with the fabulous scenery. A spotlight follows the energetic, even acrobatic solo dances, the dancers expressing their high spirits. An Indian dancer fuses Bausch's hallmark movements with elements of India's classical dance, a tradition that fascinated the choreographer.

Behind a taut plastic sheet, steam has transformed the stage into a sensual hammam. The dancers, with only towels wrapped around them, tease each other. Love and flirting are expressed in many short playful scenes; the dancers stand around as if at a party and in slow motion show off their machismo, partly by high-fiving. Later on the ensemble gather

Bathing scene from "O Dido"

Prelude to the Pina Bausch Festival 2001 with "Die sieben Todsünden" *(from left to right)*: Carmen Renate Küpper, Pina Bausch, Jan Michael Horstmann, Meret Becker, Jo Ann Endicott and Mechthild Großmann

together to celebrate under a projection of a night under the palm trees. A certain melancholy pervades the scene, though, for it is only the women who are dancing, lost and alone. *O Dido* was Pina Bausch's final work of the twentieth century, and harked back to the Tanztheater's first co-production in 1986; like *Viktor* it was made in co-operation with Teatro Argentina in Rome. But it would rarely be performed in the 21st century.

# THE WORKS OF THE 21ST CENTURY

## A celebration of life in dance (2000–2009)

Bausch's works after 2000 are characterized by a mixture of performance and dance scenes (mainly solos); sometimes dance dominates, sometimes performance. Overall the mood tends towards cheerfulness; the more harrowing content of the earlier pieces has been replaced by more conciliatory interactions between the sexes. Where beforehand every movement had to win out over an inner need, now Bausch's brand of ecstatic dance became the expression of sensual pleasures and of life itself.

For Tanztheater Wuppertal the year 2000 began with two works: in February *Kontakthof – for Ladies and Gentlemen Over 65* was staged for the first time. In May, traditionally the time for the company to premiere a new work, Bausch rang in the new century with a piece that remains in the repertoire to this day: *Wiesenland,* a co-production with the

"Wiesenland", 2000

Goethe-Institut Budapest and the Théâtre de la Ville in Paris. The foreign influences are less conspicuous than in other co-productions, save for the featured music of Hungary. The title of the piece refers to the stage set, which consists of a rock hanging in the air covered with moss and with water trickling out of it: an allegory of life and fertility, but also a fabulous and enchanted place.

With less emphasis on projections in the piece, *Wiesenland* instead prioritizes dance – mainly solos with intervening performance scenes which change rapidly and which cover a multitude of themes. A female thief is caught; a man shakes out a number of objects from her coat. Men carry a woman across the stage as if she is flying through the air. A man and a woman, both dressed in lurid colours, push a shopping trolley across the stage. A man throws wedding dresses in the air; the women try to catch them. A man slips a fur coat around a woman as if he wants to trap her in it. Women spread out their magnificent evening dresses and sway, lost in thought, as if reconnecting with themselves.

One impressive scene clarifies the intricate trails trodden by men and women: a woman crawls under or through chairs, and a man follows her carefully, whilst the tower of chairs grows and becomes ever more fragile.

After the interval the rock is brought down. The *Wiesenland* (meadow) on top can now be walked on, and becomes a paradise-like environment for a couple. Dancers, using a few planks of wood, build a kind of dwelling under the rock. A woman puts up a washing line in front. A man stations a mobile stall here, complete with portable hen-houses, perhaps an allusion to the travelling lives of the Hungarian Roma and Sinti.

A man whacks saucepan lids together, and between the beats a woman rushes into his arms. Domestic fantasies come to the fore in a huge party scene around a long table, on which all kinds of adolescent games take place. A man hops onto the middle of the laid table. The tablecloth is pulled away, even though a second man is standing on it. After this boisterous scene the dancers pair off, as if at dance lessons, and slowly bring the performance to a close.

This more cheerful phase of Pina Bausch's output perhaps reached its peak in 2001. *Agua*, a co-production with Brazil which premiered that May, is irrepressibly joyful, boisterous and colourful. Bausch grants the audience a balm for the soul: *Agua* is like a short holiday in the tropics, with sunsets, palm trees and parties. Projections magic the foreign worlds onto the stage, which consists of a closed white half-circle without any extra decoration. At one point white sofas are

pushed on for party guests who want a break from dancing the cha-cha-cha, and for a line of bathers who loll about on them flirtatiously.

Regina Advento, the Brazilian in the ensemble, dances the first of a whole series of energetic solos that belie the stupefying tropical humidity. Later on she repeatedly throws herself at the feet of the men and pulls her skirt over her face: she hides and reveals herself at the same time – playing ambiguously with the idea of sex appeal. New and promising ensemble members, such as Ana Wehsarg and Ditta Miranda Jasifi, the latter with her childlike presence, are introduced in solo dances.

Julie Shanahan holds a long monologue in the subjunctive, in which she says what she would like to do but implements it only through suggestion: she wanted to make something beautiful but it's not possible; she wanted to go mad, but it's not possible; she wanted to throw a stone through the window, etc. Her dissatisfaction and ambivalence seem self-inflicted. She does not fit in with the lively group around her

who are not interested in problems. Even Helena Pikon, too, who is somewhat surprised to discover a grey hair, remains alone with her thoughts within this young and agile group. The exuberant throng prefer to celebrate life – they cheekily spray themselves with water alongside a projection of the Iguacu waterfalls, or push each other around in wheelbarrows like gleeful children in a playground.

Regina
Advento in
"Água", 2004

In 2002, Pina Bausch created *Für die Kinder von gestern, heute und morgen* (For the children of yesterday, today, and tomorrow) without a co-operating partner. Adults who imitate children's games or who longingly recreate the light-heartedness of youth are a common theme in her work. The stage is a bare white room with over-large walls and doorways. The projections that had originally been planned were discarded shortly before the premiere, allowing instead for a sense of therapeutic concentration. During the course of the evening the walls move and the room dissolves, leaving behind a somewhat eerie set of rooms, full of shadows and hiding places.

*Für die Kinder von gestern, heute und morgen* marked a return to the Tanztheater for Lutz Förster, a dancer from its early days and its artistic director from the 2013/2014 season onwards. He is carried on by the other dancers, stiff as a board, as if asleep. Later on he provides one of the most

memorable solos in the ensemble's repertoire, in which he stands at the footlights wearing a pin-stripe suit and only moves his arms. Förster walks his fingers over his body as if playfully measuring it. He pushes his arms away and then lets them swing and turn, as if they had no strength of their own. The solo can also be seen in Wim Wenders' film *Pina*, for which the dancers repeated certain scenes for the camera, scenes they wanted to show as part of an homage to Bausch.

Like children, the men push the women up and down as if on a see-saw, play with a skipping rope, and exuberantly roll their office chairs across the stage. They often come together for group dances, whirl around wildly, sway to the music whilst sitting down or run playfully around in circles with their arms flapping. Everyone happily joins in building a sand castle, applying themselves to the task with great concentration. Two women draw hearts on the window panes, one in anatomical form, the other a symbolic expression of the different interpretations of love. Love and the quest for happiness are set out in many short

and playful scenes. Men catapult women like arrows into the arms of a man. Men alienate each other from the women: if a man is bending over a woman lying on the ground, another pulls the woman out through his legs.

In the second part the scenery becomes darker and more nightmarish, for example when the women, who are dressed in black, roughly brush their hair with a broom; or a man in a wool hat looking like an intruder tries to get from one cupboard to another. As so frequently happens, the mood swiftly changes from one scene to another; suddenly the figures seem threatening and happiness is only a vague memory. Yet the attempt to regain happiness can be rewarded, as expressed in an Indian fairy-tale told at the end: a squirrel is trying to rescue the sun which has gone missing, and although he gets burnt, he gains the ability to see in the dark and be able to fly like a bat.

The genesis of *Nefés*, created in 2003 in co-production with the Istanbul Theatre Festival and the Istanbul Foundation of Culture and Arts, dates back to 1998, when the Tanztheater toured Turkey. Its opening scene, in a steam bath, introduces

Fernando
Suels
Mendoza
and Daphnis
Kokkinos
(lying down)
in "Nefés"

us immediately to the city on the Bosphorus. A man says: 'That was me in the hammam,' as if he is looking at holiday snaps. He strikes another man – also with just a towel around his hips – with massage-type clapping actions. Then, with the help of a wet pillow, he creates some foam which he distributes across the man's back. The other men follow his example whilst the women brush their hair somewhat aggressively over the backs of the prone men in time to the drum music, so that water sprays out. The Turkish collaborators are referenced via a short bazaar scene, and a projection of Istanbul's traffic from which the women run screaming. Spaniard Nazareth Panadero compares the unfamiliar with the familiar: 'The sea is warm in the summer – like at home. The children play on the streets until midnight – like at home. It is not the same, but it is similar.' For wherever one travels, it is never that foreign there. The elements that connect cultures are bigger than those that separate them.

The wooden floor of the stage has a ditch in it, which fills imperceptibly with water until there's a small lake that can be used for all kinds of games. The wet elements underscore the sensuality that is at the foreground of *Nefés*, which in Turkish means something like 'breath'. Turkish music, sometimes slow Sufi-sounds, sometimes Turkish pop, runs through the entire piece. Individual dancers free themselves from the crowd and dance solos – sometimes withdrawn, such as Rainer Behr under the shower, or sometimes eccentrically, like the solo with breakdance positions. A female Indian dancer performs a classical kuchipudi to jazz music. The women's movements are often interrupted by the men, such as when a man disturbs a woman in the middle of her solo, grabs her by the arm and leg and spins her around before setting her back down. Another man twirls a table in a circle, and then a woman. When he sets her down, she staggers and

Melanie Maurin in "Nefés", 2003

then begins to dance again, until the men come back and pass her hurriedly over their heads.

The women give themselves childishly amusing tasks, like dipping into honey from a huge glass, or pulling a drink on a tray across the lake by a cord. They remain separate. Their contact with the men is limited and superficial: a woman washes dishes in a bucket. Occasionally she embraces a man with passion, but then returns to her housework. The ritual is repeated several times. Later the men sit on chairs and the women move like dogs, crawling towards them on all fours and letting their heads be scratched. Men come on stage in the arms of women and escape the embrace, whereupon the women stand stock still in their positions until the men slip back into their arms. At the end the men and women form a line sitting down: the men from the left, the women from the right. They push themselves forward with stiffly-angled legs, which looks complicated but which, as they traverse the stage, gains an ease.

In 2004, *Ten-Chi,* a Japanese co-production, celebrated its first night at the Wuppertal Opera House. Made in cooperation with various Japanese cultural institutions, it reflects many facets of that far-eastern country. The set shows the tail fin and back of a whale that seems to be partially protruding from the sea. The dancers move as if on a surface of water, although the stage remains dry. About one third of the way through the piece it begins to rain cherry blossoms, a shower which turns the stage into a white fairy-tale landscape.

Initially the action also seems slowed down. Short performed scenes happen as if in a trance. A female dancer lures birds with two plates, a man directs audience members in the front row as if they are about to sing for him. Mechthild Großmann recites lines of poetry about the hopelessness of love: *Als wir zwei zerfielen in Du und Ich* (As we turned into you and me). Couples dance, intertwined to music from the 1930s. But love remains an illusion in this dream world. The dancers are mainly alone with their actions. A woman tells of a dream about a prince who ran after her at the opera. Another talks about a bizarre experience in a cinema auditorium involving only her and an unfamiliar man. A woman tries to impress men with the fact that she has discovered a new star. But no one is listening.

Japanese stereotypes are examined ironically. Mechthild Großmann performs language exercises using well-known

Japanese words, such as kimono, hara-kiri, or sashimi. A dancer enthusiastically talks about the technological equipment in his house, which ranges from Sanyo to Yamaha. In contrast, Aida Vainierie develops a poetic solo to slow instrumental music. Later, she mimes being a robot, stalking across the stage making loud noises and fighting with a pillow. The second half of the evening is defined by solos from individual dancers. The swirling brightly-coloured dresses of the women against the falling snow creates an enchanted atmosphere, only occasionally broken by short performance scenes. Thusnelda Mercy carries her father Dominique Mercy on her back. He lies there on his side like an embryo: a wonderful image for the transition of the generations. The piece ends on a hectic note: the dancers run frenetically in and out of each other, repeat short solo passages, run off again, until the lights gradually go down.

*Rough Cut* (premiered in 2005) was also a co-production with Asia, this time with South Korea: the LG Arts Centre and the Goethe-Institut in Seoul. The Korean music sets up a clear reference to the country, which is then slightly belied by the staging. Set designer Peter Pabst devised an ice wall and an ice floe, which sticks out on the left-hand side of the stage. Once again Pina Bausch integrated an aspect of Wuppertal into her piece, viz members of the German Alpine Association (Elberfeld section). The familiar and unfamiliar are both present – home and abroad connect.

*Rough Cut* is full of contrasts. The cold, icy surfaces convincingly evoke a hopeless quest for love, which the

dancers explore via many short scenes. When a projection transforms the white wall into a flower-filled meadow on which a couple are caressing, it seems like a dream come true, but is curtailed by the arrival of dark figures with torches. Hectic activity alternates with moments of quiet retreat. In one long scene a projection of moonlight shimmers on the water, as men and women approach and connect with each other playfully. Some of the solos and actions of the dancers seem slowed down, as when the men perform little acrobatic tricks on small tables. They then run around and create a feeling of panic, whilst impressions of large cities transform the backdrop. A woman is thrown back and forth and then ends up hurling chairs. The themes of meditation and activity recall the piece's Asian roots. Again and again a man or a woman starts to dance as if pressed by an inner need. Michael Strecker says: 'When he wanted to become a pastor, his father advised him to join the ballet.' All the men then begin to dance and hop across the stage using dramatic arm gestures, just like classical ballet.

Melanie Maurin, Fernando Suels Mendoza and Rainer Behr in "Rough Cut", 2005

A man develops a shimmering solo by plucking paper tissues out of a box. In contrast, a woman wearing a white strapless dress like a sad bride burns paper flowers as if they were unfulfilled dreams. A man is covered in cabbage leaves like a corpse – cabbage is an important foodstuff in Korean cooking. Afterwards the women use the leaves as fans. A man holds a flame against the soles of a woman's feet with a lighter so that she has to walk faster. At the end they all run across the stage and repeat scenes or parts of their solos as if in fast-forward mode – another Pina Bausch hallmark – before the lights slowly fade.

*Vollmond* (Full Moon), which had its premiere in 2006, was created without a collaborating partner and has a relatively small cast of twelve dancers. It is reminiscent of *Arien* (1979): its dark stage also has a ditch running across it and a huge black stone at its edge, and it also features few colourful costumes. Water plays an integral part in *Vollmond*, as it does in *Arien*. In the earlier piece, the dancers also bathed in a ditch on stage and were pushed about on a lilo. In *Vollmond* the dancers joyfully pour water over themselves, slap water into each other's faces from a bucket and spit at each other with full cheeks. The women pull their hair through the water and toss it round their heads playfully. Occasionally it rains from the heavens. The ditch appears tidal, sometimes widening

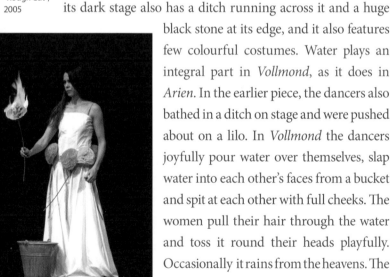

Ruth
Amarante in
"Rough Cut",
2005

out into a stream and sometimes remaining a trickle. 'This is me,' says Jorge Puerta Armenta, pulling off his shirt and dancing a wild solo. Solos interchange with impressive group dances. Whilst ecstatic dances dominate the start and the end of the piece, the middle section consists of vignettes.

The sensual piece is dominated by competitive power games between men and women. Its range of music veers from timeless 1930s works to Tom Waits and electronic pop music. But there are also still, quieter moments. A woman kisses a man demandingly like a little bird and pushes him off the stage. A woman uses a man as a wardrobe. A man pours a whole bottle of water into a glass for a woman until it overflows and she gets soaked. A man arranges a woman's long hair across his chest, while she runs her fingers through it. She fans herself with his hand.

Water games in "Vollmond", 2006

A woman requires two men for a competition: whoever can undo her bra quickest wins her favour. Caressing fingers start to scratch. A man positions a woman on the stone and fires a glass off her head with a water pistol. Whilst the women sit on chairs, the men jump up one-legged and kiss them fleetingly. Then they swap positions: coming together is a fragile balancing act.

The men and women test each other in hair-raising competitions: the men run an obstacle race across ground strewn with glass or with soft stones dropped on them from above. The women wrench their hands and legs. One sprays herself with lemon juice and groans. Another comments on this masochism with the words 'What doesn't hurt me makes me stronger.' A woman demonstrates her strength by forcing a man down onto all fours and riding him. The piece ends when the dancers unite in the water, intoxicated in motion. Despite all their differences, dance has brought them together.

For *Bamboo Blues* in 2007, the various Goethe-Instituts of India were involved as co-producers. Pina Bausch had already been to India and treasured and admired the country, but this time she was back in a professional capacity with several dancers in tow. Amongst the cast of sixteen dancers was the Indian performer Shantala Shivalingappa, who had already been a guest dancer on *O Dido* and *Nefés*. In her solos she delightfully combines steps from classical Indian dance with movements from pop music, a typical Bausch juxtaposition. She shows the audience how to tie a sari and demonstrates what cardamom smells like with the help of a perfume smelling strip. Pina Bausch expresses her impressions of India through many small vignettes, often featuring doses of irony. Two men carry a third man between them, who sits like the elephant god Danesh; his trunk made from a piece of hosepipe. Shortly afterwards, dancers skate around the stage on rollerblades.

Peter Pabst created a stage set of white curtains that blow gently in the wind. They serve as a projection screen for images of landscapes with palm trees, or enormous deities

Shantala Shivalingappa in "Bamboo Blues", 2007

Jorge Puerta
Armenta
and Anna
Wehsarg in
"Bamboo
Blues", 2007

that make the people seem very small. A game with shawls dominates the first half of the piece: they are puffed up and folded by the wind. Men wear white cloths as wraparound kurtas or as long scarves with which they attempt to capture the women. A myriad of short scenes develop against a backdrop of Indian pop music featuring drums and violins; men and women try to come together, to find each other, but always under onerous circumstances.

One man has to jump through a hula hoop in order to kiss a woman. A man and a woman slide on the floor, rolling across the stage. A woman fervently attempts to keep hold of a man in her arms. As he slips out, she starts dancing a solo, desperately beating the air with her arms. Unusually for Bausch, there are many constellations of dancers dancing together in twos and threes. A dance that starts as a solo develops into a *pas de deux* when a partner joins in, although these moments of unity are generally short-lived.

The theme of balance runs through *Bamboo Blues*. Several dancers place long branches onto the shoulders and forearms of Jorge Puerta Armenta and he walks across the stage with them. Similarly, women with balloons balance on planks set out by the men as if they were crossing some stretch of water. There is very little talking in the piece, just one lengthy scene where a man in a call centre takes monotonous orders for pizza. The search for happiness finds many different expressions, but harmony no longer appears to be just a dream.

*Sweet Mambo*, which had its premiere in 2008, could be considered a complementary piece to *Bamboo Blues*. It is performed on a similar set, made of white curtains that sway in the wind. The programme notes say that the piece is an attempt to see 'how two different pieces can be developed with different dancers but from the same starting point'. The results are genuinely very different. Whilst in *Bamboo Blues* there is hardly any talking, *Sweet Mambo* is reminiscent of Bausch's earlier works. In many short monologues the dancers state their individual backgrounds. 'My name is Regina, not said with a g but with a sh,' says Brazilian dancer Regina Advento, and orders the audience 'not to forget'. During the course of the performance other dancers follow her example, as if they wish to make their identities official. Most of the dancers in *Sweet Mambo* are long-term ensemble members, in contrast with the predominantly younger cast of *Bamboo Blues*.

Regina Advento in "Sweet Mambo", 2008

The cast consists of three men and six women, and it is the women who shape the evening – the men are more like assistants. Nazareth Panadero, in a blonde wig, repeatedly walks up to the microphone and screeches hysterically. Her life motto, 'Life is like riding a bike, either you travel or you fall,' seems more like a corny joke. Later on she confesses, 'When I'm not feeling well, I prefer to complain in Spanish.'

In a party scene, just as everyone is standing with their glasses at the ready, Julie Anne Stanzak reveals how to conjure up the best party smile: just say 'brush'.

Whilst the men and women get close to each other or manipulate each other in different variations, the film *The Blue Fox* with Zarah Leander runs in the background; it too is about love, jealousy and new combinations of couples. This is also what the dancers are seeking, sometimes delicately and playfully, sometimes more aggressively. A man runs in circles around a woman; she holds tightly onto her dress and hair. Two men prevent a woman from approaching her friend; again and again they catch her as she's running, then carry her back, yelling, to the start. When the men want to rub their faces on naked skin, the women only expose their backs.

The curtains act as useful props for games of hide and seek or create comfortable hollows in which the women can lie down to rest. At one point in the second half, which contains more dance content, a curtain suddenly blows across from the right and creates a huge bubble in which a female performer dances a spectacular solo in silhouette. One woman asks a man, in her own version of sign language, whether he has time for her, clumsily attempting a direct translation of language and feelings into dance and gesture – something Pina Bausch never did.

Whether or not Pina Bausch knew that 2009 would bring her last work – on that we can only speculate – there is nothing to suggest the end was near in the work itself, which was packed with celebration and vitality. Premiered on 13 June, ...*como el musguito en la piedra,*

Couples in "Sweet Mambo", 2008

"...como el musguito en la piedra, ay si, si, si ...", 2009

*ay si, si si ...*, a co-production with Chile (specifically, the Festival Internacional de Teatro Santiago a Mil and the Goethe-Institut), premiered on 13 June 2009. It was given its official title posthumously by her partner, Ronald Kay, and comes from a song 'Volver a los 17' by Chilean songwriter Violetta Parra.

The younger dancers feature in this piece, which celebrates dance and vitality in a series of partly introverted and partly ecstatic solos. Only Dominique Mercy stands out of the crowd, at sixty years old embodying life's sense of wisdom and serenity. At one point he lets himself fall and a younger dancer catches him – a conciliatory image of young and old. All of the dancers, with Mercy at the front, sit across the stage in a line and ruffle each other's hair, celebrating this harmony between generations.

If *Bamboo Blues* contains allusions to Indian stereotypes and clichés, the Chilean piece in contrast holds back from direct references and portrays only universal images. There are a few clear references: South American music, including pan-flutes, and a man in a poncho with a knitted hat. The mood is mainly a cheerful one, and the battle between the sexes is less severe. The women dominate again.

Whilst the men in their dark suits appear to be uniformly similar, the women in bright, flowing evening dresses exude aplomb.

Right from the start the women are hassled by the men, carried around like objects and then plonked down again. A woman has to run like a horse in harness, another tries to escape but is held back by a rope around her hips. Yet gradually all becomes more conciliatory: solos develop into duets and relaxed ensemble scenes. There is kissing and hugging. Playing the role of Latin lover to the full, Fernando Suels Mendoza rhapsodizes in glowing tones about one particular woman – until the next one comes along. The most disconcerting moments are provided by the set, which consists of a white floor like a sheet of ice. Now and then, the floor opens up to reveal jagged-edged chasms, before closing again.

Clémentine Deluy in "... como el musguito en la piedra, ay si, si, si ...", 2009

And, for the last time, there are water games, men in women's dresses, dancers addressing the audience, animals. All Bausch hallmarks. As her last work, it suggests a possible direction for future projects: a celebration of life through dance as a contrast to everyday problems. 'You know I learned to enjoy the moment – and you know I like it!' one dancer says. Just ten days after the premiere, Pina Bausch died in a hospital in Wuppertal.

Tsai-Chin Yu in "...como el musguito en la piedra, ay si, si, si ...", 2009

# THE ENSEMBLE

## 'I'm interested in the personality'

'It is a love affair, not just a working relationship, which can sometimes lead to suffering',[1] said the dancer Ruth Amarante about her relationship with her principal, Pina Bausch. Since the Tanztheater's inception in 1973, more than 150 dancers have been part of the company, usually with around thirty dancers at any one time. Some leave and return later, others leave for good, and have to be replaced. Finding new dancers was a demanding task since Bausch looked for unique personalities: 'Of course I want very good dancers with a good technique. But actually I'm more interested in the character.

Pina Bausch in conversation with her ensemble during rehearsals in the Lichtburg, 1982

I rely on my gut feeling. I always like it when people make me curious.'[2]

Pina Bausch proved to have a particular gift when it came to choosing ensemble members: she looked for strongly charismatic dancers with stage presence and charm. Their physical appearance was less of a factor. Dancers came from all over the world to audition for her, to have the chance of becoming part of the famous company. Multicultural was not simply a word but a daily reality for the twenty-nine dancers from seventeen different countries. All of them brought their own personalities, mental attitudes and cultural background to the works, which is why the universal language of the work is understood the world over.

Dominique Mercy, Jan Minarik, Nazareth Panadero, Helena Pikon, Malou Airaudo, Beatrice Libonati, Jean-Laurent Sasportes, Meryl Tankard, Jo Ann Endicott, Lutz Förster, Ed Kortlandt, Anne Martin, Urs Kaufmann, Monika Sagon, Marlis Alt, Julie Shanahan, Julie Anne Stanzak – the list goes on. All are strong protagonists without whom the early years of the Tanztheater would have been inconceivable. 'They all had a strong impact on the Tanztheater,' said Pina Bausch. 'It was a very mixed group with different qualities; something about each individual moved me. I was curious about something, something I didn't know.'

An actress with a distinctive deep voice, Mechthild Großmann, an ensemble member from 1979 and still a guest performer even today, held an unusual role in the group. 'She was an unbelievable authority for me,'[3] Großmann said of

Pina Bausch. 'She possessed the energy and the toughness required to run a company for so many years.' During her life there was no one else with whom Großmann spent so much time. She describes the relationship of Pina Bausch to women as follows: 'Pina had a lot of respect for men, more than I did. She knew the women. Which is why we women were lucky enough to have many complicated roles and, apart from in very few pieces, the lead roles. She looked at women differently from the way she looked at men.'[5]

The longest-serving dancers are now practically of pensionable age, but this gives the works an extra and unusual edge. Someone who, for example, saw the revival of *Two Cigarettes in the Dark* in May 2011, experienced how well the younger dancers, such as Eddie Martinez and Tsai-Chin Yu, harmonized with the older dancers, such as Dominique Mercy and Jakob Andersen, and how much each generation inspired the other. It is a combination that has few equivalents in the dance world. Ensemble mainstay since 1979, Nazareth Panadero, the Spaniard with the raspy voice, called it: 'A mixture of being old and being a child.'[6]

'Pina was a painter, and we were the colours,'[7] is what dancer Andrey Berezin said. Each person could, in fact had to, bring something of themselves. Perhaps some felt manipulated by this process and left the ensemble, but others welcomed the fact they were not treated as marionettes by choreographers, performing only what was conceived for them. With Pina Bausch, they could contribute their own ideas, their own personalities. 'I think they are all people who like to give a lot,'[8] she once said of her dancers. This kind of work requires great trust, but in the end both sides are rewarded. 'You are suddenly allowed to do things that you don't do in life,' said Jan Minarik, 'like in a wondrous dream.'[9] Malou Airaudo even felt that if Bausch called her an angel, then you believe 'you are more than human'.[10]

It would not be strictly accurate to view everything that a dancer says on stage as an expression of their own personality, not least because many roles have now been re-cast – although as Pina Bausch pointed out, '… we don't perform like actors perform a role in a pre-determined play, instead we play ourselves, we are the piece'. But whereas it was this authenticity that was striking in earlier times, nowadays it is the tension between the role and the persona that is part of the appeal. Bausch's intention, after all, was not to present something 'private', but rather to convey something universally recognizable in an individual, which the audience could re-discover in themselves. 'I love my dancers,' said Bausch, 'each in their own fashion. It is dear to my heart that one can really get to know these people on stage. I find it really lovely if, at the end of the performance, one feels closer to each of them because they have revealed something of themselves.'[11]

In the early years it was hard to imagine that roles could be passed on to other dancers. Yet over the course of the years it became a routine, which generally worked well. Jan Minarik, the only dancer Bausch inherited from the ensemble of her predecessor, Ivan Sertic, left a huge gap when he departed.

Fortunately, Michael Strecker, Andrey Berezin and others have been skilful replacements. Bausch says: 'Of course it is very difficult when dancers leave the company to find someone who can take over the different roles. One thinks of course of certain qualities, but one doesn't find the same person again.'[12]

When choosing her dancers, Pina Bausch preferred certain types: the women are mainly pale and have long hair, which when they dance, swings with them as a flowing part of a movement. Indeed, Jo Ann Endicott writes in her book about Pina Bausch's disappointment when she cut her hair short.[13] The choreographer did not look for specifically beautiful dancers, but for strongly-expressive ones. When it came to the men she often went for dark-haired, southern-seeming types who could translate their temperament into movement. Meanwhile, the blonde-haired members of the ensemble (such as Lutz Förster, Michael Strecker or Andrey Berezin) formed a contrast. They could all be short or tall, fat or thin, what was important was presence.

In the 1990s, the ensemble welcomed a number of important new members. People such as Ruth Amarante, Regina Advento, Rainer Behr, Aida Vainieri, Cristiana Morganti or Fernando Suels Mendoza, whose personalities would strongly shape the works of the noughties and perhaps helped make the atmosphere of the productions more cheerful and life-affirming. 'I considered it to be important that something of the special qualities of these dancers flowed into the work,'[14] Pina Bausch said.

The youngest generation of dancers, such as Jorge Puerta Armenta, Pablo Aran Gimeno, Ditta Miranda Jasjfi, Kenji Takagi, Clémentine Deluy, Aleš Čuček, Tsai-Chin Yu and Thusnelda Mercy dance and move with ebullient joy, marking their choreographer's last works with their intoxicating solos. 'The young ones bring with them a breath of fresh air,' Bausch explained in 2004. 'They have all influenced the pieces because they love to dance. A sort of ambition sets in.'[15] Works such as … *como el musguito en la piedra, ay si, si si…*, which opened only days before Bausch passed away, display the captivating power of dance. Since then, even more dancers have joined the ensemble who never knew Pina; at the start of the 2015/2016 season there were already eleven new dancers in the ensemble, and there is no doubt that this rejuvenation process will continue. Interest in the company is not waning: in the spring of 2015 alone, 1,200 dancers from around the world applied to audition.

The choreographer demanded a lot from her dancers – she was strict, uncompromising, and stuck to her guns. 'It was never easy to work with Pina,' writes Jo Ann Endicott, 'each time it was a challenge.'[16] But Pina Bausch also had a huge heart, as Mechthild Groβmann recalls: 'Pina was very, very considerate – also of the personal issues of individuals, in a way that is not otherwise found in theatre.'

# THE SET DESIGNERS

## 'Seeing things as if for the first time'

When set designer Peter Pabst began collaborating with Pina Bausch, it all started with a deer. For *1980* Pabst emptied the theatre completely and covered the floor with turf. The audience sat on the meadow, exactly like the deer. Pabst designed practically every set for the Tanztheater for twenty-nine years and his natural floor coverings and unusual landscape architecture on stage ensures that each work remains unique. Sometimes the choreographer even named the work after the set design, for example *Nelken* (Carnations), *Das Stück mit dem Schiff* (The Piece with the Ship) or *Wiesenland* (Meadowland).

Nazareth Panadero in "1980"

The composition of a stage floor is particularly important for a dance piece – the flow of movement is determined by slopes, elevations, sand, earth, salt or water. Rolf Borzik was the first who dared to attempt these unusual experiments: he created the turf floor for *Rite of Spring*; for *Arien* he set the stage underwater; he covered the floor with wilted leaves for *Bluebeard*. He ensured that there were constant new challenges for the technical crews of Wuppertal's opera house and theatre. Following the death of Borzik, Gralf-Edzard Habben (*Bandoneon,* 1980) and Ulrich Bergfelder (*Walzer,* 1982) each designed a set for Bausch, but it was Pabst and Bausch's artistic symbiosis that endured until the choreographer's death. Pabst had previously worked with Peter Zadek at the Schauspielhaus in Bochum, which is where he met Pina Bausch in 1978, and where he stretched the boundaries of possibility for set designers even further.

'When it comes to my set designs I have to find a unique artistic form,' Pabst explained. 'Natural materials are just the right thing because, in biological terms, they have wonderful shapes. And they are contrary because actually they do not belong in a theatre, in an artificial space. Water does not belong in a theatre and causes huge problems. Natural materials are suitable for dance theatre because they are warm, sensual. And dance theatre is a highly sensual affair.'[1] The naturalistic worlds that he devised, together with the exposed stage mechanics which on the whole were kept visible, create a delightful contrast to the sensuality of the dance. 'If you bring something into a theatre that usually belongs outside,' said Bausch, 'then that opens people's eyes. Suddenly they see things they thought they knew in a new way, as if for the first time ... These things preoccupy their senses and mean that they stop thinking and begin to feel.'[2]

In a long interview with Wim Wenders, Pabst recalled how his distinctive set designs came into being, and how he oversaw the research, the painstaking testing of materials and the technical construction. The grass for *1980* had to be regularly watered, aired and mown, the 8,000 artificial flowers for *Nelken* were specially made in Bangkok, and *Palermo Palermo*'s collapsing wall could only be constructed of hollow bricks made of wood shavings dipped in cement, so that they were not too heavy but could remain stable. He covered the floating island in *Ein Trauerspiel* with blast-furnace slag because 'it sparkled ... like milled glass'.[3] In *Das Stück mit dem Schiff* he had the ship become stranded on a sand dune. For *Der Fensterputzer* he built a movable mountain of roses and Hong Kong bauhinia – the flowers on that territory's coat of arms; for *Vollmond*, a river flowed around a stony landscape; for *Masurca Fogo,* cooling lava flowed into a room; for *Ten Chi,* a whale fin rose out of the ground. For the snowy landscape of *Tanzabend II* (Madrid) Pabst obtained a special kind of Epsom salts that did not burn the dancers' feet, while for *Ahnen* he created models of the giant cacti using a confectioner's piping bag and then got the Wuppertal stage workshops to copy them.

Regina
Advento
and the
crocodiles in
"Keuschheits-
legende"

In *Ahnen* a walrus enters between the cacti, one of several animal performers who take a role in the Tanztheater's works. In *Arien*, Jo Ann Endicott dances a love affair with a hippopotamus, in *Keuschheitslegende,* she walks a crocodile on a leash, and in *Nelken,* men with German Shepherd dogs patrol around the field of flowers. They provide a provocative counterpoint to seemingly idyllic worlds and epitomize how familiar things can become alien in a different context.

Along with his creations of surreal pictorial worlds, Peter Pabst also designed bare sets that he himself ironically named his 'Zen pieces', such as *Nefés*, or the Chilean piece *… como el musguito en la piedra, ay si, si si…* in which he and Pina Bausch consciously eskewed any kind of illustration and made only sparing use of props. The great phase of using projections started with the Madrid piece *Tanzabend*

*II*, in 1991. The cold white salt landscape was an effective projection screen which could transform into hot deserts, idyllic flower meadows or disaster scenarios. In *Danzón*, the set is made up of tulle curtains and a projection screen onto which an ever-changing series of moving and still images are projected. The dancers blend in to become part of these strange yet familiar worlds. Pina Bausch herself danced in front of one film, featuring tropical fish that Peter Pabst had filmed in an aquarium. In *Água,* the co-production with Brazil, colourful projections of people dancing, wild animals and jungle scenes create a lively atmosphere and reflect the South American attitude to life. Yet the set designs, despite all their playfulness, never become merely decorative or folkloric in reflecting the co-producing countries. Pabst says: 'The cities that invite us often have very concrete expectations of how one should react to a place. However, we do not show either bitterness or beauty as such at a documentary level. It is a world of its own. Only one thing is important for the set design: whether it helps the dancers to tell their stories, not whether or not it gives a likeness of a city.'[5]

What also makes the Tanztheater's sets unusual is their longevity. After a theatre run, of two years at most, scenery is usually either put into storage or shredded. With Pina Bausch, every prop or piece of scenery is saved. This means the work can be revived easily. And what's more, the sets must be adaptable for other stage spaces, as the theatres around the world that receive dance theatre tours have widely differing configurations. This is taken into consideration right at the start. *Bamboo Blues,* for example, was destined to tour to India, so it was practicable for the technology 'not to become too complex,' Pabst remembers. The stage set, which consisted of white curtains that moved in the wind, were used again for the following work *Sweet Mambo.* It worked in terms of content as well, because Pina Bausch had decided to create a new production on the same theme but with different dancers. Unlike the colourful (Indian) projections, in *Sweet Mambo* the videos are mainly monochrome. Peter Pabst frequently accompanied the Tanztheater on its tours so that the sets could be set up on foreign stages with the same level of care and attention to detail employed at home.

Pabst did not allow effects to be overused and changed his aesthetic means of expression so that the sets would not become uniform; the process of creation was always an adventure. 'When Pina Bausch started rehearsals there was nothing,' remembers Pabst, 'no theme, no text, no music, no title, which meant that for a designer there was initially nothing to design.'[6] He visited rehearsals frequently in order to gain an impression of what the new work could be about. Only then did he begin to develop several drafts and present them to Bausch. 'And then we began to discuss and ask ourselves,' he explained, 'what it would mean if this scene took place in this world or another

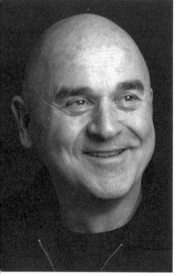

Peter Pabst

one. That is an interesting exercise, because you notice that the environment has a huge influence.'[7]

'Pina, like no one else,' Pabst said, 'could recognize the possibilities of a set design, compare it with her own requirements and see how to use it for herself and the dancers – all in a matter of moments.'[8] Frequently the set design was developed alongside the work right up to the first night. For example, at the final rehearsals for *Bandoneon*, at one point the onstage rehearsals were running overtime so the stage crew started to take down the scenery (designed by Gralf Edzard Habben), and by the end the dancers were dancing on an empty stage. Pina Bausch liked this so much that she incorporated it into the piece, building it into the first half before the interval. In *Für die Kinder von gestern, heute und morgen,* all the videos that had been prepared for the work were never actually shown.

This meant that the dancers had to familiarize themselves with the set just a few days before the premiere and learn how to deal with the specifics of it. Pabst says: 'I'm afraid that the majority of dance companies would have chased me out of the building if I had presented them with what I have expected Pina's dancers to put up with over the course of our twenty-nine years together. I have thrown enough stones at them in my time, and sometimes even boulders.'[9]

# THE COSTUMES

## The unmistakable style of the Tanztheater

Rolf Borzik had been responsible for both scenery and costumes in Bausch's productions, but after his death in early 1980, Peter Pabst took over as set designer while Marion Cito became costume designer for the next production, *1980*. Cito had been a dancer and member of the Tanztheater company since 1976. She had danced in *Bluebeard, Komm tanz mit mir* and *Renate wandert aus* and had worked as assistant to Bausch before devoting herself to the costume department, so she knew how Bausch worked and had a very clear understanding of her demands.

Marion Cito making up Pina Bausch in the wardrobe of the Teatro Real Madrid, 1998

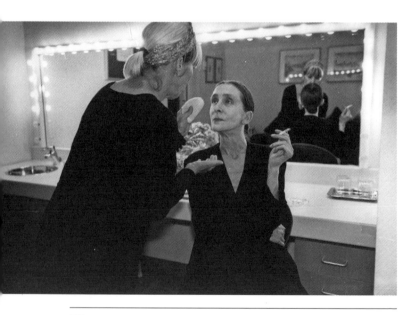

Cito further developed Borzik's achievements in costume design. Whilst the male dancers of the Tanztheater usually appeared in dark suits or just in shirt and trousers, simple and unobtrusive, Cito dressed the female dancers – according to the mood of the piece – in colourful dresses. The dresses frequently served as a mirror to emotions. It is Cito we must thank for the extravagant evening dresses which highlight a dancer's elegance and lend their movements a vibrant sensuality. She left an indelible mark on the unmistakeable style of the company. No other choreographer dared dressing their dancers in evening wear without risking being associated with the Wuppertal ensemble.

Pina Bausch did not like disguise. It was her aim 'not to want to stand out, not to be transported away, not to disguise oneself … the people on stage must be recognizable as people, not just as dancers. In order not to disturb the performance, I want them to be seen as people who dance.'[1] While the dancers' costumes could hardly be described as everyday clothes, they gave the performers room to reveal their individuality. Often the festive evening wear creates an atmosphere similar to that of a ball, so that the dancers show themselves as refined night time guests, but with cracks in their smooth façades. The way the men and women attack or play childish games contrasts with the civilized superficiality of the costumes. In some works, such as *Viktor, Palermo Palermo* and *Masurco Foga*, the female dancers wear light summer or strappy dresses, not dissimilar to nightdresses, which make the dancers appear vulnerable.

Personal taste clearly played a large part in the choice of colours and materials. Marion Cito sought new and intriguing materials from around the world which she then presented to Bausch and had tailored into costumes. Cito frequently oriented her work towards the individual dancers: 'At the beginning we have nothing, no piece, no set, nothing. We only have a cast. That is why I work very personally. I have a pool of materials and I consider what would best suit who, and only then does it go to the costume makers.'[2] During rehearsals there were often dresses, either bought or tailored, hanging up, ready for a dancer to try on.

When it came to co-productions, Cito looked for materials associated with the relevant country. Although each dress was to be individual, the colours had to work together, for example in a scene in which all the women of the ensemble dance in a line. The dresses were a unique part of the production, and that meant that they could not simply be used for other works. In *Danzón* there is a playful exchange of dresses: two women bend forward, grab hold of each other's arms, the men pull the dress from one woman to the other over their heads, as if it were double-sided. Helena Pikon's dress plays a specific role in *Sweet Mambo*: the flowing shimmering material is so blown about by the wind that the dress seems to dance as much as the dancer – the effect is fascinating. For Marion Cito it was always important that the costumes serve the dance, that they don't constrict the dancers' movements, thus arms are often left bare.

Disguises, perhaps to develop grotesque characters, were always anchored to the action and developed during rehearsals. These included Jan Minarik (and his replacements) as the Statue of Liberty with a diadem made of cigarettes, as a giant baby, or as a dog owner with a white fur collar and cigarette holder: the absurd outfit and the corresponding exaggeration of the character frequently inject humour into a piece. Men in women's dresses and role reversals create distance, as in *The Seven Deadly Sins*, *Nelken* or *Bamboo Blues*, as well as challenging stereotypes. 'I love men in dresses,' Cito admits, 'and I always have a selection of dresses at hand.'[3]

Pablo Aran Gimeno in "Bamboo Blues", 2008

# THE MUSIC

## A collage of contrasts

Pina Bausch was not a choreographer who set something to music. The scenes and movement sequences were created first, without music or with only 'background music pieces', which were the work of two musical collaborators, Matthias Burkert and Andreas Eisenschneider. These were pieces of music that created a particular atmosphere; they were not intrusive, but acted as a neutral counterpoint to the material that was being rehearsed. For the solos, Bausch and her musical collaborators only added the music once the material was ready, unlike other choreographers who developed dances to particular compositions. Bausch wanted the movement to come from the depths of the dancers; she wanted them to listen to their own musicality and not to follow a pre-determined rhythm. Pianist Matthias Burkert, responsible for the music at the Tanztheater since 1980, said that Bausch did not want 'the music to completely support what the dance was already saying.'[1]

As one scene follows another in a piece, a musical collage gradually takes shape, comes together, often as contrasting sequences: extremely slow sounds or silence follow quick rhythms, rock music follows renaissance music, electronic rhythms follow African drumming, or the Comedian Harmonists come in after Mozart's *Eine kleine Nachtmusik*. A dynamic dance can gain a completely different dimension if the music works completely against it. 'Suddenly one understands the music through the dance, and the other way around,' Burkert explains. And that is the ideal situation.

This collage-like soundtrack was style-defining for the Tanztheater, each time the mix of old and new music was a gamble. Bausch developed her works using this technique from early in her career. Whilst *Iphigenie auf Tauris* (1974) and *Orpheus und Eurydike* (1975) followed scores by Christoph Williband Gluck. By 1977 she had started moving away from firmly established musical scores, as in *Blaubart – beim Anhören einer Tonbandaufnahme von Béla Bartók*. Instead, the music was chopped up, played forward and backwards, and some passages were repeated. In her next piece, *Komm tanz mit mir* (1977), she used a variety of folk songs that were sung by the dancers themselves but which nevertheless formed a stylistic entity.

The musical collage technique was fully adopted by Bausch at the end of 1977 for *Renate wandert aus*, which consisted of a mixture of hit songs and evergreens. The styles of music used became more eclectic: in *Kontakthof* (1978) there was music by Juan Llosas and others, while compositions from the 1920s to the 1940s were frequently heard in Bausch's works.

In the earlier works there were many periods of silence, from the late 1980s onwards the musical collages became uninterrupted, and the musical collaborators tried to reflect the music of the co-producing country. That began with *Viktor* (1986) which featured music from the various regions of Italy. Naturally there was Korean music in *Rough Cut*

(2005) and Indian music in *Bamboo Blues* (2007). But the soundtracks never became folkloric; there was consistently an unusual combination of music, the choice and compilation always surprised. It was a working method that would inspire other choreographers.

During rehearsals, the team would try out a broad selection of music until Bausch felt something was right. Sometimes a particular piece of music might suit one dance but then not fit the overall context of a production, but this might not become apparent until the final rehearsals. If that happened, Burkert and Eisenschneider would have to start their search anew. With each production using thirty to forty different pieces of music, the archive now contains several thousand tracks. It was very rare that a piece of music was played to the end in a work. Precisely when and which section of a piece of music was played in and out was always down to the choreographer. That was her secret. 'Pina Bausch was a deeply musical person without knowing much about the theory of music', said Burkert. She made her decisions based on her emotions: 'Sometimes it breaks one's heart. Sometimes you know, sometimes you find it, sometimes you have to forget everything and start all over again. One has to be very alert, sensitive and receptive; there is no system.'[2]

The main task for Bausch's musical team was research. They sought new works and unusual tracks, met musicians and composers and searched archives. Local research was particularly important for international co-productions. Sometimes the pair also recorded sounds and ambience

*left:* Matthias Burkert; *right:* Andreas Eisenschneider

in a host country. They collected plenty of material so that they would have a selection ready for the rehearsals. Each dancer also had their own selection of music. 'When I hear a piece of music,' explained Burkert, 'I think, for example: "That is something for Dominique Mercy."' After so many years the musical team knew the dancers well and so it was not difficult to allocate. A certain amount of courage was required in suggesting a piece of music to Pina Bausch. 'I knew it could all go horribly wrong if I offered the wrong thing,' added Burkert. 'It would mean the dancer would be influenced in a different way.'

Bausch once said that the music had to be so effective that it still gave her goosebumps on the 250th hearing. If there were signs of fatigue during rehearsals, as during preparations for *Für die Kinder von gestern, heute und morgen*, she would allow her colleagues free reign to bring in other music not used until that point. 'We once had a romantic flirty scene,' Matthias Burkert recalled, 'and previously had accompanied it with romantic flirty music, so we simply tried something completely different. The music was raw and sinister. It was very refreshing and just completely cleared everyone's head. All at once this led to wonderful scenes, some of which remained in the finished piece.' This experience showed him that 'when the music changes one's experience is transformed. Music changes everything and allows it to be seen in a completely different light.'

Pina Bausch's taste in music was completely open. 'Theoretically, everything was possible', Burkert said. If something suited the moment for the choreographer, then it was right. Over the last ten years of Bausch's life, however, there was a major shift in the musical content of the Tanztheater's pieces. This was attributed to the influence of Andreas Eisenschneider. Whereas the company's previous output had been shaped by Burkert's specialist background in classical music, world music and jazz, Eisenschneider introduced contemporary music, electronic compositions and rock and pop, which opened completely new doors. Bausch's mind always remained open. 'Her openness to any kind of music was certainly astonishing for someone nearly in their seventies', commented Burkert. Over the years her taste had grown alongside theirs.

Pina Bausch had a very precise ear for sounds. Burkert reports that if dancers wore different shoes, she noticed this immediately by the way they sounded. The way Dominique Mercy scratched the earth with a shovel in *Auf dem Gebirge hat man ein Geschrie gehört* always had to sound the same, which was particularly difficult when touring and performing on foreign stages.

# DEATH, FUNERAL AND REMEMBRANCE

## Pina Bausch's spirit will live on

'Pina was a scientist, a researcher, a pioneer of the blank spots in the human soul.' At Bausch's memorial service on 4 September 2009, film director Wim Wenders' eulogy emphasized her inimitably precise way of looking at things. Nearly 800 guests gathered at the Wuppertal Opera House to say goodbye to an extraordinary woman. As well as Wenders, prominent fellow travellers included Pedro Almodóvar, choreographers Alain Platel, Anne Teresa de Keersmaeker, Sasha Waltz and Susanne Linke, Christina Rau, wife of the late President Johannes Rau, governor Jürgen Rüttgers, and many others. Despite the drizzling rain, several hundred hangers-on had gathered in the Engels-Garten next door to the opera house to pay their last respects. They were able to follow the talks and dances in the opera house via a live relay on a large screen. A sense of grief and loss was written across the faces of everyone who had to come to Wuppertal that morning, their tears mixing with the rain.

The unexpected death of Pina Bausch, the creator of dance theatre, on 30 June 2009, just two weeks after her last premiere, had come as a complete shock. Newspapers all around the world reported the news, many with photos on the front page. Outside the German press it was notably the French papers who dedicated long obituaries to a choreographer who had visited their country so many times. In her homeland, the President of the time, Horst Köhler, called her 'an excellent

Pina Bausch's grave

representative of the cultural nation that is Germany', while John Neumeier, artistic director of the Hamburg Ballet, said that Pina Bausch had 'shaken up everyone in the dance scene and ensured that everyone examined the honesty of their own work'. Choreographer Martin Schläpfer thought that her death was a 'wound that will perhaps never heal'. For Vladimir Malakhov, artistic director of the Staatsballett Berlin, she was a 'wonderful person' and 'one of the most influential artists of our times, who also influenced theatre directors'. Lastly, Bausch's colleague Johann Kresnik described her as 'an icon of Germany'. These were some of the many tributes quoted from the 3Sat television channel's *Hommage an Pina Bausch*.

Her private funeral took place at the beginning of July. She was laid to rest in the reformed evangelical cemetery of Varresbeck in Wuppertal-Elberfeld near the person who discovered her, Arno Wüstenhöfer. Mountains of wreaths and flowers lined her simple grave, situated in the middle of a wood looking out over a small pond. Since then the grave has been marked by a plain plaque on a monolith. Fans have laid plastic carnations and little angels there.

At her remembrance service, at the Wuppertal opera house in September 2009, the dancers of the Tanztheater ensemble performed a selection of scenes from her expansive body of work, their bodies and movements expressing Pina Bausch's philosophy not through the medium of words but of dance. Their choreographer had given her all, to the point of exhaustion. 'She did not economize with her gift,' Wim Wenders said in his eulogy. 'The greatest art of all when dealing with people, I think, is to get the best out of them and make it visible. This is what Pina mastered.' Furthermore, Wenders went on, the dancers had been 'the orchestra of Pina's expression'. He called on the political decision-makers present at the service to continue to promote and back 'the work and the legacy, yes, the global legacy of Pina Bausch's Wuppertal Tanztheater'.

Guests at the memorial service in the opera house, 4 September 2009

That same autumn, in 2009, Wenders began to make a film tribute to Bausch. *Pina* had its premiere at the Berlinale in 2011. Since then it has delighted more than half a million cinema-goers across Germany. It was the first documentary film to be made in 3D, and through his new 3D technology, Wenders created a brilliant way of adapting choreography for the cinema screen and conveying its stunning sensuality. Some scenes show Pina herself, talking, or – as in *Café Müller* – dancing. Her dancers' contributions reflect a deep reverence for her as both artist and person. The film highlighted one certainty: the spirit of Pina Bausch will live on.

# THE LEGACY OF PINA BAUSCH

## A perspective

'Once I was sitting with a gypsy family in Greece. We sat together and chatted, and then at some point they started to dance, and I was supposed to dance too. I had huge inhibitions and a feeling of "I can't do this". Then a young girl came up to me, maybe twelve years old, and demanded again and again that I dance with them. She said: "Dance, dance, otherwise we are lost…" Pina Bausch recounted this story when she received the Kyoto Prize in 2007. It clarified the significance that dance held for her; it was a necessity, as important as breathing.

The dancers carry on Pina's work and continue to dance, dance, dance, the way they danced on the day their 'mother' and mentor died. It was not self-evident that the company would continue to exist after the choreographer's sudden death, nor that the dancers would continue. Initially there were no new productions; instead the old works were performed and partly re-cast – for the first time without the choreographer being there. Dominique Mercy and Robert Sturm became joint artistic directors until the end of the 2012/13 season, and tried to continue to lead the company in the spirit of their deceased artistic director.

It was clear to those in charge, however, that at some stage there would have to be a new production under another choreographer. Introducing a new line-up would take time. It was only at the beginning of the 2015/16 season that three new, short works came to be rehearsed, which would make use of all thirty-four dancers. Internationally-renowned choreographers were chosen: Tim Etchells and Theo Clinkard (Great Britain), and the artistic duo Cecilia Bengolea (Argentina) and François Chaignaud (France). The three-part evening, weighted with high expectation, was described as a 'gentle first step' towards the future by Alistair Spalding. Spalding, artistic director and chief executive of Sadler's Wells in London, together with Stefan Hilterhaus, (PACT Zollverein, Essen) and Myriam De Clopper (deSingel, Antwerp), advised Tanztheater Wuppertal on this process of change. In the meantime, a solution for the successor to Lutz Förster has been found: as of the 2016/2017 season the company will have have two people at its head. Dirk Hesse is to become managing director, whilst the new artistic director is Adolphe Binder, previously artistic director of Operans Danskompani in Göteborg, Sweden. It is unlikely that the company will only work with one choreographer. As Lutz Förster says: 'There will not be a new Pina Bausch for Wuppertal.'

The footprint left by Pina Bausch is huge and impossible to fill. Any successor would have to let go of her model in order to develop her ideas. There are several of her former dancers who have turned to choreography in the interim, amongst them Jean-Laurent Sasportes, Malou Airaudo, Meryl Tankard, Rainer Behr, Fabien Prioville and Mark Sieczkarek. In February 2011 some dancers from the

Tanztheater presented their own choreographies under the banner *Carte Blanche* at Café Ada in Wuppertal. It was a successful experiment.

A series of evening events entitled *Pina Underground* took place in various venues outside the opera house (the zoo, business premises, a car park) and revealed the potential of individual dancers as choreographers. The relatively small framework of the performances meant the evenings had a workshop-like character and were not intended to mark any kind of new beginning.

The Pina Bausch Foundation, which takes care of maintaining both the choreographer's legacy and spreading her influence, was set up in her memory by her son, Salomon Bausch. Now, he and Madeline Ritter form its board of trustees, along with Christian Koch as managing director. The Foundation is supported financially by the state of North Rhine-Westphalia, the Kulturstiftung des Bundes, and the Jackstädt Foundation Wuppertal. As the copyright owner of Pina Bausch's choreographies and works, the Foundation aims to keep the artist's memory alive by maintaining an archive accessible to the public. It was Salomon Bausch's wish, in line with his mother's lifelong connection to Wuppertal, to find a place in the city that would act as both a memorial and an archive, as well as an interdisciplinary centre for study and research, for dancers and young choreographers to experiment with dance theatre. And a place has been found – the Schauspielhaus – which, with federal, state and civic help, could develop into a Pina Bausch Centre. A decision on this has yet to be made, nevertheless, the city, state and the federal government have already made two million Euros available as development monies for the project to take it up to 2016.

As a fleeting performative event, dance theatre only finds its true integrity live on stage. Thus it is important to examine, catalogue and preserve its canon, so that the works can be revived at any time. During her life Pina Bausch decreed how the materials should be archived and accessed, namely by reference to the work in chronological order. 'From the beginning, the care and use of an archive was an essential part of my mother's work,' Salomon Bausch explained. 'For several years she, together with a number of dancers, pursued the systematic indexing of the growing portfolio, in particular many thousands of video recordings. She set out precisely what belonged in an archive, and what structure that archive should have.' The materials do not simply document Pina's work; they are also the prerequisite for looking after the works. Vital to this, Bausch added, is a 'living archive', in other words the knowledge and experience of the Tanztheater's dancers and employees, along with their personal memories and experiences. And so Marc Wagenbach, who works at the Pina Bausch Foundation, developed an oral history project: in 2011, following performances of *Two Cigarettes in the Dark*, seven audience members interviewed seven members of the Tanztheater company – working either front or backstage – for seven minutes. These forty-nine conversations brought to light some very personal memories and the project is scheduled to be repeated in a similar fashion with other pieces. For *Du und Pina*, citizens of Wuppertal were invited to share their memories of Pina Bausch.

At the time of writing, the Foundation is based in Pina Bausch's former flat on Fingscheid in Wuppertal-Unterbarmen. The archive comprises material on fifty-three works: show-bibles, notebooks, scores, set and costume sketches, photos, technical directions, props and costumes, some of which are still occasionally needed for performances. On top of that there are thousands of programmes, posters and press cuttings, over 35,000 reviews, as well as countless

Members of the ensemble in conversation with audience members at the "Oral History" Project, 2011

photos. Personal correspondence, letters, speeches, prizes and interviews complete the collection.

Since 2007 the thousands of video recordings have been watched, catalogued and digitalized by dancers Bénédict Billiet, Barbara Kaufmann and, right at the start, Jo Ann Endicott, working in accordance with the parameters set out by Bausch herself. Undertaking the task of archiving are Gigori Chakhov (video) and Ismaël Dia (digitalization), with 38,000 photos already digitalized at the time of writing.

The oldest videos are from the 1970s. Since then video formats have changed constantly, and over time have become less and less readable. This is why all the videos are to be digitalized so that they can be reproduced at any time. It is hugely time-consuming as the process must run in real-time. The recordings form an important basis for the future of Pina Bausch's works. Eventually, specific videos will be made publicly available.

Working together with the Hochschule Darmstadt, the Pina Bausch Foundation is developing a huge database of 3,900 costumes. The aim is not only to gather information on the material and cut, but all the costumes, along with their details and measurements and a colour reference table, are

Digitalizing videos for the Pina Bausch Foundation

to be photographed from the front and back. The sets will be documented with sketches, photographs, samples of material and text. If the original plans are no longer available, then new measurements will be compiled and translated into layouts, views, sections and detailed drawings.

The Lord Mayor of Wuppertal, Peter Jung, explains that there is still no square or street named after Pina Bausch, the city's citizen of honour, as no suitable place has yet been found: 'It has to be somewhere special with charisma.' In Solingen, Bausch's place of birth, no agreement could be reached about re-naming a square, although the foyer of its civic theatre is to be renamed the Pina Bausch Foyer. Even so, the Friends of Pina Bausch, founded in 2010, aim to compile and document all traces of her life in Solingen. In 2015 they unveiled a plaque on the former Café Müller in central Solingen, which today is a chemist. Meanwhile, at a ceremony in October 2009, the old auditorium at the Folkwang Hochschule in Essen, in which Pina Bausch once danced and which the choreographer had been responsible for maintaining since 1988, was re-named the Pina Bausch Theatre. It was a fitting tribute, since Pina Bausch was connected to Folkwang for over fifty years.

Surely more important than these tributes is the continuation of her work through other artists. She did not merely make her mark on the next generations of choreographers, she also influenced opera and theatre directors, wittingly or unwittingly, with her way of mixing up the genres, such as comedy and tragedy, of moving action from the individual to the general and thus to the whole ensemble, and of translating the battle of the sexes into powerful scenes. Pina Bausch led the way with her quasi-documentary theatre, that explored the human condition with targeted questions, and which created art out of personal material taken from her performer's wealth of experiences.

Wim Wenders' documentary film *Pina* continues to ensure that Bausch's legacy is disseminated and enters the mainstream. Its Oscar nomination brought unforeseen publicity for the Wuppertal ensemble. Across the globe audiences are able to gain an impression of what moved Pina Bausch, the sensuality of her dance, and what her human 'theatre of experience' can provoke. She is certain to inspire people for a long time to come, to bless them with her work,

Celebrating the Tanztheater Wuppertal Pina Bausch, 1998

and to make them think. She shows how important it is to have courage, to follow your own path, to follow your intuition – and to follow your dreams.

It is in her work that Pina Bausch lives on.

# INTERVIEWS

## 'I always want to open a new door.'

Pina Bausch interview with Marion Meyer and Frank Scurla, 10 October 1998, as part of the celebrations of the twenty-five-year anniversary of the Tanztheater:

*Twenty-five years of the Tanztheater: what was the greatest success, the most moving moment, and the most important confirmation?*

There are not just individual things. There are so many wonderful experiences, many small things that one is so

happy about. There is so much I have developed with the dancers. There has been continuous development, even in the audience's response. I have always experienced the most moving moments with the dancers. I was so happy if we had a great performance, for example in Istanbul. The fact that our time spent in Wuppertal already adds up to twenty-five years is moving. And that we travel around the entire world, that people ask us to come back. That we create connections between there and here. That people open their doors to us and let us partake in their culture – for me it is a duty and challenge to continue doing so. One should not rest on one's laurels.

*Do you have favourite choreographies? Or are there pieces that you would no longer stage?*

I do not have a favourite work, because each piece has something to do with the time that it was created. It is like a child being born: you give everything. And like with children, one loves them all equally. The consideration always has to be: what piece is one going to perform and where? People from different cultures also react very differently. The pieces consist of open scenes that one can read a great deal into. *Fritz* is the only one I'd be scared of seeing again. Initially that was also the case with *Iphigenie*. Even though it was so close it was still so distant. Every work has many colours. I am curious and always want to open a new door.

*What does dance mean for you? Has your understanding of dance changed over the years? What influences were there?*

The Folkwangschule and Kurt Jooss certainly influenced me greatly. There was a specific atmosphere there. All the artists were occupied with something in a different sort of way. Equal value was given to the basic training in classical and modern dance. Jooss' style always had to do with humanity. There was a mixture of cultures, everyone was about the work. Then in America I learnt a lot more. That was a crazily inspiring time. I felt as if I was at home there. The development of dance – that's a difficult thing. Certain themes come suddenly to the fore. One is always thinking: what is dance? The strongest expression is the body. One cannot express anything better. But the form has to be right; one has to ask where a feeling comes from. Each individual person in a work is important for me. I have to find something for everyone.

*There are bound to be difficulties if someone has to be replaced?*

Everything has to do with the person who is performing. If that person is replaced, it becomes just a role. Then another has to find their way into it, until it is theirs. That usually takes a long time, until it is right. In some pieces I had to set the tasks afresh. Then sometimes it becomes better. To change work retrospectively is not on. Only to shorten it. One can't retrospectively paint over a finished picture.

*Over recent years your works have become more cheerful. Has your view of things become milder over the years?*

My works are always both: cheerful and sad. The works live by contrary feelings. Cheerfulness is always based on something. Perhaps it's very much needed at present? One always has to find a balance. It is important that one laughs together with the audience. And in many different countries people laugh in the same place.

*After virtually every performance you go up on stage for the applause. What does applause mean to you?*

[Laughs] When someone boos I think it's even more important to go on stage. I pledge myself to my ensemble. I then feel something quite beautiful with the dancers who are on stage. I always attend the performances.

*Can you separate the private from the professional?*

It is difficult to separate them. Both are very important to me, both flow into each other. I cannot separate myself from myself. If I am thinking about a piece, however, I do have to be alone.

*What do you look for in your dancers?*

I take note of body and technique, but primarily I engage a person who dances. It has something to do with a feeling. I am interested in something about that person. I want to learn something from them, have new experiences. It is a mutually enriching thing. Why that person in particular? That is something I can only feel.

*There have always been attempts to woo you away. What kept you in Wuppertal? What does that city have in particular?*

At the beginning there were practical reasons. The travel was arranged well in advance, the planning done two years ahead. We always committed ourselves and had no time to worry about it. Besides, I appreciate both houses in Wuppertal. They are wonderful stages, in particular the opera house with its audience-stage set up. In Wuppertal, theatre is part of everyday life, and that always had a great attraction for me. The relationship to reality, too – it is important to remain grounded. There are a whole host of reasons why Wuppertal is special. It is always lovely to come back.

# DOMINIQUE MERCY INTERVIEW

## 'Pina never rested on her laurels.'

*Can you still remember how you met Pina Bausch for the first time?*

I received an invitation to go to Sarratoga in the USA in order to perform in a piece. I spoke very little English, no German, and Pina had no French. So we didn't speak a lot to each other. We looked at each other and thought that we'd probably understand each other. There was an immediate connection there that did not require many words.

*Did you go directly to Wuppertal with her?*

Shortly before I left she was standing in the kitchen talking about, amongst other things, her new project. 'If it becomes concrete, would you work with me?' And I said: 'Of course.' I was very aware that, in her, I had got to know someone very special. What I've experienced, discovered, I would never have been able to develop with the company in France where I was engaged at the time. The boundaries there were too narrow.

*Did you ever think you'd become the longest-serving dancer?*

No. I never thought that I would dance for so long, that I would still be in Wuppertal, or that I would still carry some responsibility for the Tanztheater. Over time it has sort of happened that one just keeps on going.

*How would you describe your relationship to Pina Bausch?*

I believe that first friendship has remained. Pina always has a very personal relationship to everyone, on different levels. I think that I belonged to those who had a closer connection to her. What I perhaps regret is that I never took that step to be completely on Pina's side, which would have meant being there for her morning, noon and night. I was always aware that I had a certain responsibility towards Pina and the company, but at some stage I also felt that I needed some distance too. When Pina asked myself and Lutz Förster to give lessons at the Folkwang-Hochschule I was uncertain at first, but then I noticed that it was such a lot of fun. I needed more time for myself, a certain distance.

*Were you able to give her any advice?*

We had a good and constructive relationship. She often involved me in decisions on casting or re-casting. She also wanted me to be there for the auditions. I gave my opinion. But in the end Pina always did what she felt was the right thing. Thank God! At first I didn't understand. But she asked so that she herself could be clearer about things. It took some time before I understood that this was the right way of scrutinising oneself.

*Was there a quality that you particularly valued in her?*

Yes, several. I found her strength extraordinary. Her consistent work. She had the energy to do things in parallel. She was nearly always present at rehearsals, and between rehearsals she was in the office. When it came to a new work she would think about it until 2 a.m. and sleep very little. She just kept on going. I respected that. I admired her beauty, her elegance, her patience, her openness.

*Was there anything about her you didn't like?*

Early on I sometimes had the feeling that she was like a spoiled child. And of course she was not.

*Did she change over the course of the years? You did work together for over forty years.*

Of course, but she changed because the conditions did. The company got bigger and bigger and, with it, the responsibility grew. No matter how famous Pina got, she never took anything for granted. She was never secure, she never rested on her laurels, never, never. But life of course changed her. At the start she was not a mother – she had more time to go out to eat after rehearsals. Later on in Wuppertal she would always go home after rehearsals.

*How would you explain the fact that the works over her last decade were more cheerful?*

I think that also had something to do with it. It is easy to forget that she started in Wuppertal aged thirty-three. By her last piece she was almost sixty-nine. I think that one's views, one's sensibilities towards the world, are bound to change. And at certain intervals the company renewed itself and younger dancers arrived, who brought with them a different energy, a different power, different movement qualities that Pina incorporated. Over time she gave the dancers more freedom. Pina frequently said that she made her happiest works when she herself was at her saddest. And only someone who has reached a certain maturity can do that.

*You danced in Pina Bausch's last work in which many young dancers are on the stage. Did you feel a bit like a mentor?*

No. But with some scenes I did say to Pina: 'I do feel odd here, as if I don't belong.' And she recognized that and took me out of that scene.

*How do you feel now in your position as co-artistic director?*

I think that it is like many things in life: it all takes time. Robert Sturm and I did not want to replace Pina. We had to find a way of carrying on sailing this boat together with the dancers. Doubt and difficulty are all part of it, but I do feel in the right place.

*At some stage will there be the possibility of a new direction?*

I think we have to allow ourselves time. That is a creative process, until everyone is in place. But of course we have to start doing something. We're talking a lot about it and thinking it all over. It is still too early to talk about it publicly.

*You also have to ensure that the company stays together?*

Yes, of course. Everyone recognizes the importance of our work and they all want to be part of it. That is extremely valuable. Whether in the office or in the ballet hall – the company is important to everyone.

*Would you revive a piece that Pina Bausch herself never re-programmed, such as* Renate wandert aus *or* Fritz?

No, I don't think so. In different conditions it could perhaps happen at some point. But I rather think not. For Pina *Fritz* no longer belonged in the repertoire. *Renate* was in fact never completed. She watched the piece a few times on video together with the dancers. She felt like doing it again. It wasn't going to stay in the drawer for perpetuity. The only problem was that she did want to revive some pieces but not in their present condition. She wanted to work on them. Cut things. That is the ethical question: what to do now? Now I believe we can no longer intervene. We do not have the right to tweak something, even if Pina had planned to do so. That is the question, whether at some point we decide to show the piece anyway. Let's see.

*Will there ever be a dance festival again under the umbrella of the Tanztheater? Or was that associated with her as a person?*

It all started as an anniversary event in 1998. And then came the second festival in 2001. And because it was so beautiful and colourful, it attracted people from all over the region. That is why she was asked if she wanted to become artistic director of the International Tanzfestival NRW. It was wonderful to create a NRW festival in 2004 and 2008 with so many artists from home and abroad, but it took a lot out of her. Pina is not someone who does things by halves, although of course she had helpers. For us alone it would probably be too difficult, but what the future will bring, we can't say that at the moment.

*In your daily life and work, what is missing the most without Pina Bausch there?*

Pina. I can't say anymore. She is missed, by all.

*What is Pina Bausch's legacy?*

I can't read the future. I don't know how long we can keep the works alive. And even if the pieces are no longer performed, the whole thing is still somehow there. What this person gave to culture will not be forgotten for a long time. Architects, theatre and film makers – she influenced people on all sides.

*If you could speak to her now or ask her something, what would you say to her or ask her?*

Oh, now I'd have a lot to ask. I've got a whole list: Pina, can you help me? Tell me, what is the best way to do this? I would love to be as organized as she was. She always said she couldn't manage otherwise. That's what I've still got to learn. I would ask her: how do you do that?

---

**Dominique Mercy,** born 1950 in Mauzac, France, worked from 1965 onwards at the Grand Théâtre in Bordeaux and in 1968 was engaged by the newly-founded Ballet Théâtre Contemporain in Amiens. In 1971 he met Pina Bausch during the Saratoga Summer Festival in the USA. Two years later she engaged him for her newly-formed Tanztheater. Here he quickly developed into one of the most outstanding and defining dance personalities, whose creative role-development characterized so many works. Following Pina's death in 2009, Dominique Mercy and Robert Sturm took over as co-artistic directors of Tanztheater Wuppertal.

# JO ANN ENDICOTT INTERVIEW

## 'Not a day goes by that I don't think of her.'

*In your book,* Waiting for Pina, *you write that it was love at first sight when you first met Pina Bausch. What fascinated you so much?*

Her face, her eyes – that direct first glance that bored into you, her elegance and charisma! Her simple beauty, she wore no make-up. At the time I was selling tickets at Covent Garden. That evening I showed her to her place, she was wearing a wonderfully simple black velvet dress and took long strides. I saw that she had long hands.

*Did you speak to her?*

She spoke to me. She had been watching a training session at the Dance Centre in Covent Garden. She was looking for dancers from across the globe for the opening in Wuppertal. She asked me if I'd like to come to Wuppertal as a soloist. At the time I was a bit plump, but that didn't worry her. Up until then in my dancer's life, I'd always heard: 'A couple of kilos less would be good.' 'Have some teeth removed so that your face has more shape.' That's terrible. She accepted me without wanting to change me. She saw that I was a good dancer.

*What did she say?*

She talked about what she wanted to do in Wuppertal, not so much about ballet. She wanted to find a new way together with us, the dancers. She was interested in everything, particularly what moved us as people, combined with all our skills: more acting, pantomime, singing. The more you could offer, the better. That interested me. It was never boring. There was always something new to add to the mix. You were allowed to act, scream, weep, laugh, to do everything with her – frequently to physical and mental limits.

*Did you ever feel any doubt?*

No. I always believed in us. The word trust was very important.

*What happened with* Blaubart? *Wasn't there a kind of crisis between Pina Bausch and the ensemble?*

Yes, many didn't want to go on dancing. In the earlier works there was not so much dancing. The dancers who didn't get a chance left. *Blaubart* is a difficult piece with a lot of brutality. We started with questions and answers. Pina did not give us the steps for the choreography, but the start came through her questions to us. Her questions were very intimate, private. Our replies gave away a part of our inner-lives. Through the constant musical repetition of the events in a scene, the piece became more intense, more aggressive, more brutal. It's like being at the dentist. It's torment. Although it is a brilliant piece. The piece nearly finished me. Pina asked a lot of us.

*There were also reactions from the audience: what happened at the first night of the* Macbeth *piece in Bochum?*

The Shakespeare Society had expected to see *Macbeth*. But the piece is called *Er nimmt sie an der Hand und führt sie in das Schloss, Die anderen folgen* (He Takes Her by the Hand and Leads Her into the Castle, the Others Follow). At the beginning we were all lying down on the stage and not much was happening. We were doing different sleeping positions. The audience started rampaging and booing. They were restless, disruptive and not concentrating. So I suddenly stood up and said: 'If you're not interested, then go home and watch television, but let us get on with the work!' And I left the stage. When I came back on, I carried on with my refrain from the piece: 'Help me get away.'

*That was quite spontaneous?*

Yes, it was very courageous of me. Pina thought it was wonderful that I did that. I was just so annoyed.

*What is it like talking to the audience? One never knows what might happen...*

I always loved playing with the audience. I'm a spontaneous and temperamental person. Often I don't know beforehand what I might say to the audience. It is my gift to feel and to react. And so everything remains fresh and alive. We are people on a stage who can dance and act. Because of the themes of the piece we had to deal with each other. It was always exciting standing on stage in one of Pina's pieces.

*If you had to describe Pina Bausch, is there a term you can think of spontaneously?*

Magical. Unique. Secretive. She had an aura, a simplicity. But she wasn't easy. Multi-layered. Generous. But also difficult. A wonderful dancer, a brilliant choreographer. When one works for so many years so intensively, so close up, then things get squeezed. It is quite normal that sometimes there is friction.

*What qualities did you not like about her?*

She did not learn that sometimes enough is enough. There are boundaries. We are all 'only' human. She did not spare herself.

*One didn't feel put under pressure?*

Not really. If she asked questions and you didn't have an answer, you weren't forced. But I knew her so well that I'd notice if she wasn't satisfied.

*One gets the impression from reading your book that your relationship with Pina Bausch was a kind of love-hate relationship …*

I've always been very emotional. I think the pieces would not have turned out as they did if I hadn't been. I can't perform something in the pieces and then be different in my private life. I have very many feelings and one has to accept how I am. At the time I said: she is a vampire.

*What was it like, if there was an argument?*

One apologized, or one didn't speak for a whole week, and then things just carried on. One could always solve the problems within the work. I don't bear a grudge. Actually we got on really well. I always tried to take the pressure off her. When I left, well then, I noticed I was empty. Besides, I had a family that needed me too. But when I left, I never really left Pina – in my thoughts I was always there. Even today not a day goes by without me thinking of her. Unfortunately. I still need some time to get over it. She defined my life for so long.

*Did Pina Bausch not need a break?*

Everyone needs a break. Pina too, but she was unstoppable. I don't know anyone who worked as hard as Pina. Always thinking about her Tanztheater. And if you said to Pina: 'I can't go on,' then she'd reply: 'I only know one thing: the best solution to all problems is to continue working.'

*Is that what you meant when you described her in your book as 'detached'?*

Yes, her pieces are so human, reveal so much about feelings, relationships, experiences, wanting-to-be-loved, a game between childhood, adulthood, and death. I think at some stage her feet were no longer touching the ground.

*Over recent years the pieces were more joyful in their colours and music: how do you explain that?*

Yes, they are beautiful and have power. Pina did not stand still. It came about through the co-productions. She adapted to her dancers and remained faithful to them and to her own path. I could imagine that she became increasingly content with each piece. At present I'm avoiding watching Tanztheater pieces, because every piece brings its own memories, and that's not good for me.

*What is it like handing on a role to someone else?*

Peculiar. Particularly if they're leading roles that you have played all your life – it hurts. All of my characters contained some of my secrets. You then have to impart them to someone else. It's a little like betrayal. But it has to be like that because I can't go on performing in the pieces forever. I'll soon be sixty-one years old. I last danced *'Komm tanz mit mir'* in Japan at sixty, and it was really great. I performed and danced with such passion because I knew that it was my last performance as a dancer. I suddenly understood all those love songs. I felt that Pina's spirit was there.

*What is it like to be able to dance on stage at that age?*

Wonderful – you perform every time with another kind of longing. At the same time, it's painful, because you know your life as a dancer is nearly over. You dance with a different kind of passion. You know your role so well because after thirty years it has become a part of you. Dancing was the most precious thing I ever had, particularly in old age.

*What do you think Pina Bausch's legacy is?*

Oh, so much – the works and the dancers who are still there. She lives on in her pieces more than ever. The Foundation is the future. Everything that Pina put into the world goes on. She remains unforgettable. What she achieved is enormous. She is a 'wonder of the world'.

---

**Jo Ann Endicott**, born 1950 in Sydney, initially studied classical ballet and ended up dancing in the Australian Ballet Company before she met Pina Bausch in London in 1973. Bausch engaged her as a solo artist for her new ensemble in Wuppertal where, over the first decades, she decisively influenced the pieces. In 1987 she left the company to devote herself to her family. In 1994 she returned as a guest performer, to run rehearsals, and to be Pina Bausch's assistant. She rehearsed, amongst other things, *Kontakthof with Ladies and Gentlemen over 65* and *Kontakthof with Teenagers over 14,* as well as the Bausch pieces at the Paris Opera.

---

# JEAN-LAURENT SASPORTES INTERVIEW

## 'She sees everything, even that which is not seeable.'

*You joined Pina Bausch's company in 1979 – what was your experience of the mood of the ensemble?*

At the time the company was still not so well-known but the character of the dancers was very, very strong. What I saw during rehearsals was impressive. I was like a small child that has suddenly been locked in a toy shop overnight. I was overjoyed.

*Was it clear at the time that you would be heading in a new direction in Wuppertal?*

I didn't know exactly what I was looking for. I'd never seen this way of speaking before. Pina said the things that I wished I had said myself. And afterwards it was clear: this is a perfect fit.

*How was it in the rehearsals: did she always have a whole raft of questions ready? Or did she also ask questions spontaneously?*

I think it was both. She was prepared inside, but she was also very intuitive. She was like a sponge, and it was all working away inside her. She was always open. One could tell that a lot of her questions were influenced by everyday life.

*And she also referred to previous rehearsals?*

Yes, exactly. If someone had offered something that made her think, or gave her a new idea. There were also misunderstandings. Then someone else would understand a question quite differently. Someone answers with something that doesn't fit the question at all ends up opening a new door.

*There was already something like a theme or a basic idea? Did the dancers know what it was all about?*

We knew nothing and we never spoke about it. It was not necessary. Every day we would have new questions and one could gradually see and feel what direction it was going in. I believe it is dangerous for creativity to understand too much. Because then you try to serve what you think you had understood. That limits the imagination. For her it was certainly clearer, but we never spoke about it.

*To begin with, were you all in the rehearsals?*

Yes, it was like being at school. Everyone brought in a notepad and a pen. And then we got the questions and began to imagine. Each person for themselves. Although we could use someone else to create a scene. Nor was it a problem if we needed more time either. We got four to ten questions a day, so we didn't have to wait long. They quickly piled up. We got about 100 questions per work.

During this phase Pina was working about twenty hours a day. Then she looked at the material she had, and arranged it. She might only use individual elements and then integrate them into another context. She did the building phase in parallel. And then she began rehearsing and blocking the scenes in different variations.

*Did she always decide what would be done and how? Or could one as a dancer also say, actually I think this is more beautiful?*

No, not that. She was the one who created the work. We could always offer ideas if she wanted to choose between two or three parallel scenes. She was completely open to listening and trying it out. But she had the final say.

*Was she strict?*

I wouldn't use that word. She demanded a lot from her dancers but demanded a lot more from herself. She was not strict. She always reacted very humanely. She also had a way of getting what she wanted that worked very well.

*Was she patient?*

Very. Particularly in comparison with other choreographers and directors.

*When the pressure increased just before a first night, did the mood change then?*

Very quickly I got used to that. For me a premiere was not so important. The work was never finished. And the pieces sometimes changed drastically afterwards, usually during the first week. Of course there was a lot of tension before the premiere, with Pina too, because she had worked so hard. She became very tired and tense.

*What was it like in the 1980s when success hit? Did you not find that a bit odd?*

No. There had always been people who found the work great and people who thought it was terrible. We experienced that particularly sharply during this time. In Wuppertal they threw tomatoes and vegetables at us during *Bandoneon*. Sometimes the doors were slammed – that is still the case, it's just that the ratio has gradually changed. But even when we performed *Nelken* in Salzburg in 2005, one could sense that the endurance threshold was not so high. There were people in the audience who were used to something more conventional.

*Did that make the dancers feel unsure?*

I don't think so. It always made me a bit edgy. I was convinced by the quality of Pina's work. Sometimes we even had audience members come on stage. In *Keuschheitslegende* a man came onto the stage and sat down in my chair. Once the scene was over, I took him back to his seat. In *Bandoneon* Nazareth was standing on stage and reading a poem. A member of the audience came on stage. When Nazareth went off, the man took a bucket of water that was standing around and emptied it into the audience saying: 'I had the impression I needed to do something.'

*Did the success change the work?*

No, I think success only ensured that we had more technical possibilities. Pina was not influenced by success. She was very self-critical.

*And the company, did they change?*

No, I think Pina only engaged people who were interested in the work and not in their position. One is so taken up with the piece, with the questions that are being asked. Despite the huge success the dancers remained self-effacing. That had a lot to do with Pina.

*Did the pressure increase because of the success?*

Not so much for the dancers, because Pina carried the whole responsibility. I think, for her, the tension and the stress did increase.

*Did she ever let the dancers feel it?*

I think that the stress and the pressure was not external. The question always was: what is the best way I can say what is important, what I want to say? That was her biggest stress. She was only working on the fundamental, not on what came from the outside. The internal world was important to her, where you want to go to create a work.

*What would you say about her humour?*

She was very sensitive and alert when it came to humour in a piece. Jan Minarik had an incredible feeling for humour; one can see that in his scenes. As soon as he proposed something, she integrated it into the piece.

*Did she laugh a lot herself?*

Yes, a lot.

*How do you view the new pieces?*

With a great deal of understanding. We spoke about them. She had the feeling that she had already said so much about certain themes in different forms that the world now needed more positive energy. There are so many terrible things around that she wanted to present the audience with a positive feeling about being alive, and not hold up a harsh mirror, as in previous works. That is legitimate. I personally am more moved by works such as *Blaubart* or *Palermo* than I am by the later pieces that contain much more dance.

*What do you think Pina Bausch's legacy is?*

Much more than one thinks. Her influence on other dancers is huge, on choreographers, directors too. That will continue to be the case. I hope that the company will survive and that the theatre will remain the company's home. The demand from the public across the world is huge. Remains huge. One needs a space that is alive in which her work is carried on, in which other choreographers can also work with the company. It would be a real shame not to continue to use the gift. Meanwhile there are many dancers in the company who also choreograph. There's still a lot to happen if we are given the chance.

---

**Jean-Laurent Sasportes**, born 1952 in Casablanca, studied dance with Anne Marie Porras (jazz), Peter Goss, Hans Züllig, Jean Cébron (modern dance), Nina Vyroubova and Suzanne Oussov (ballet). He joined the Tanztheater Wuppertal in 1979 as a solo dancer. After leaving the company he remained faithful to Pina Bausch's ensemble as a guest performer. Since 1996 he has worked as a freelance dancer, choreographer and teacher for, amongst others, directors Yoshi Oida and Burkhard C. Kosminski, for both opera and theatre. In 2005 he founded the Ikonoklast Dance Festival in Wuppertal, which took place for the fourth time in 2011 at Café Ada. He teaches kinomichi in Germany and Japan. Since 2014 he has been working in France with people with a mental disability, and in Wuppertal with people with autism.

# THUSNELDA MERCY INTERVIEW

## 'One has to be very precise – very Pina.'

*As the daughter of dancers Dominique Mercy and Malou Airaudo you were, so to speak, the first child of the company.*

Yes, and I still am – and that is something very special, that in such a large company there is a continuing generation.

*What was it like for you as a child, did you attend a lot of rehearsals?*

Yes, I found it all very exciting with the dancers, my present-day colleagues. After school I'd race to the opera house and see the last few minutes of rehearsals. I knew virtually all the productions by heart. It is nearly all connected to very

positive memories, apart from the times when I had to stay behind in Wuppertal with a babysitter whilst the company and my parents were away on tour. I understood, however, how important it was to them and how very much it belonged to our lives.

*How do you remember Pina Bausch from when you were small?*

She was already friends with my parents by the time I was born. She was like family, even if we didn't see each other so much privately. The relationship only changed when I joined the company as a dancer. Then of course it was not only familial, but there was work to be done.

*What was the first rehearsal with Pina Bausch like?*

Terrifying! During that first rehearsal my emotions went up and down. I had the feeling that everyone was looking at me. The whole love towards Pina as an artist, as a person, was overwhelming. One felt really very small – it was hard to live up to that.

*Was she strict?*

Yes, she was strict, and she had to be. It is not about doing someone a favour if one dances or develops a piece of work. One has to be strict in order to take people beyond their own boundaries. I think she knew exactly what she wanted. She had this incredible gaze and perspective which she used to see where each individual could go. And I think she knew that she was the key for leading each individual there in an individual way.

*That requires an instinctive feeling for so many people with different mentalities?*

We are very different people with different desires, problems, longings. You have to be very diplomatic, very precise – very Pina.

*Is there another adjective that might describe Pina Bausch?*

Generous. She gave everything of herself, for her work, for her dancers. She invested her time in the company and in her work and yet never lost her connection to the world outside.

*Was her generosity also an incentive to give more of oneself?*

Absolutely. For me she was and is a role model for power, discipline, precision, for intuition and very good timing. She had an incredible feeling for the right moment.

*When did you become a permanent member of the company?*

2003. My first production was *Ten Chi*.

*Did you go on the research trip for the productions?*

Not to Japan for *Ten Chi*, nor to Korea for *Rough Cut*, the Korean co-production. But I was in India for *Bamboo Blues* and in Chile for the last piece.

*Did you get any sense of which impressions would eventually flow into the piece?*

Everything was possible … the things that I thought would definitely go in were very rarely used. We speculated amongst ourselves, but Pina kept it to herself till the end, until the piece was finished in her eyes. And then we, and the audience, could discover it on stage.

*What were rehearsals like after the trips? Did Pina Bausch refer back to the research?*

Pina asked questions in relation to the country, sometimes concrete questions and sometimes she left them wide open and one could take what one wanted. In Chile we travelled around discovering things whilst also rehearsing. We could react directly to something. Not in India – there, we were mainly on a voyage of discovery and then brought our inspiration back to the studio in Wuppertal.

*In terms of the Indian piece, can you remember something concrete, something that remained in the piece?*

Many things can be found in the movements in my dance that came out of the questions she asked us during improvisations. One question was about people and animals. I sat against the wall and moved only my painted arm like a snake, and later on she integrated this movement into my dance. Or a picture of those plants in the water, anemones, that are so long and entwine themselves around everything: the short duet that Damiano and I performed was inspired by that image – we are intertwined. Different unforeseeable things, people, places can inspire and stimulate us.

*How does a solo dance then develop?*

It varies. Usually the material is gathered, even filmed, and then we watch it with Pina, she comments and everything is written up in terms of the information gathered. And then you're filmed again, and the movements commented on, and so it goes on. It developed like that, with individual commentaries from Pina. By the end you have a longish dance section which only then is put on stage. And then the music is added. Different kinds of music are tried out, even if it still doesn't have the form or the mood that Pina is looking for. The creation of each solo is individual to each person.

*How many pieces have you danced in? Including the ones you took over?*

Many. Some of them have a very particular meaning to me. In *Bandoneon* I danced my mother's role, that was very intense. I'd already seen the piece a lot in my childhood, and we were all a bit surprised because in this role I look very much like my mother. There are so many wonderful and interesting works: *Keuschheitslegende, Nelken, The Rite of Spring, Kontakthof, Fensterputzer* and *Áqua, Palermo Palermo* and and and ... every work has quite particular and personal memories for me.

*Were you in all the new works after 2003?*

I didn't do *Vollmond* and I assisted on *Sweet Mambo*. Pina asked me. That was an honour. I am very happy I was able to have this experience – a very intimate, special and important experience to see how a work is created from the outside. You get a completely different perspective when you watch how people dance, argue, live on stage from the outside. And the next time that I stood on stage myself, I had a different understanding of the whole.

*What were your tasks?*

To accompany the rehearsal process, to write everything down in terms of what the dancers were showing in the improvisations. Where they come in from. Even if everything is recorded on video, it was the kind of record where things could be looked up quickly. For example, what music was played when, or the colour of a dress.

*That is collaborating very closely with Pina Bausch? How did you find that?*

Fantastic. Intense. Because I was so close to Pina in a different way, I could appreciate her differently. It is simply another kind of proximity. And artistically it is very valuable, to accompany her to a certain point, to see things the way she sees things and how she brings it all together.

*Did you gain more of an insight?*

In some ways, yes. I had her perspective from the outside. And I tried to follow it with her, to feel it with her. But I didn't have any influence on the piece. That was her thing.

*Were you ever asked as her assistant what you found to be better?*

No, it was never about what is better, only she could know that. Sometimes I could give my opinion or my perceptions, but the decisions were always made by her.

---

**Thusnelda Mercy**, born 1977 in Marseille, grew up in Wuppertal. While studying at the Folkwang University of the Arts she worked as a dancer and actress with Theater der Klänge, and as an assistant to the choreographers Kuo-Chu Wu and Juan Kruz de Garaio Esnaola. She was a permanent member of the Tanztheater Wuppertal ensemble from 2003 to 2015. She was engaged by Sasha Waltz in 2002 for the creation of *noBody* and in 2015 for the revival of *Roméo & Juliette* in Berlin. In 2009 she founded the trio CDT with Clémentine Deluy and Damiano Ottavio Bigi. They presented their own works as well as pieces by guest choreographers, including *Herbst* (Autumn) by Malou Airaudo in 2009 and *SAMUEL-titre de travail* by Pascal Merighi in 2015, which toured Germany, Italy, India, Argentina and Chile. Since then she has been teaching modern dance and composition/improvisation. In 2013 she presented her solo *Agrégat* at the DANSFabrik festival, directed by Lucas Manganelli. In 2013 she took over as artistic director of the festival series BACHIBOUZOUK together with Mare e.V. She also took part in the 2014 BACHIBOUZOUK-Special as dancer and assistant, directed by Pascal Merighi.

# LUTZ FÖRSTER INTERVIEW

'Maintaining the pieces is an active and creative process. It is not *museum work*.'

*You first came to Wuppertal as a student for* The Rite of Spring. *How did that come about?*

I didn't start dancing at Folkwang until I was twenty-one. Everyone said I was too old and too tall, apart from the head of the dance department, Hans Züllig. At some point Züllig said to me: Frau Bausch has her eye on you. She had seen me in *Tanzabend* and needed students to expand the male contingent in the cast of *Spring*. I was there because she wanted to have the tall blonde guy with the big nose and the lovely second position. The name Pina Bausch didn't mean

anything to me at the time, but because of that, after just one year of my training, I had the opportunity to appear with a professional company in an opera house! The first thing I noticed about Pina Bausch, and this was a first for me, was that she spoke like both my grandmothers – with a local Solingen accent.

*What was the company like back then?*

The company was completely different. There were still a lot of dancers who had sort of landed in Wuppertal by chance. If something didn't work she blamed me, the student beginner. But Pina Bausch dealt with everyone equally, whether they were famous guests or young students. All that counted was whether something was correct or not. That gave me courage.

*You became a permanent member of the ensemble in 1978.*

It was an exciting time. I threw myself into it completely, and as a result, didn't always make myself popular. There were times when I was the most hated member of the company. I wasn't always easy.

*Because you always said what you were thinking?*

Yes, it was a long journey from my early career to my present position.

*How would you describe your relationship to Pina Bausch?*

I think it was a great friendship. A very great relationship based on trust.

PINA BAUSCH

**Pina Bausch dancing jazz in 1973 at an event at the Wuppertal opera house**

*What did you learn from her?*

I think that I had already learnt a lot in Essen and discovered that Pina and I are cut from the same cloth. Folkwang stands for a certain way of teaching dance. Later on when I came to teach at the Folkwang University I formulated it like this: we do not train dancers, but people who dance. The person is at the forefront. It's all about dealing honestly with movement. But what I actually learnt from her and what I still benefit from, is patience. That woman was unbelievably patient. I have never seen anyone who was so unflustered, no matter what the situation. Intuitively she spoke very quietly, but also deliberately, so that people came to her. She gave people time to grow, to try things out. She was very precise. And also her criticism was very unflustered – but persistent. Pina was always completely concentrated on what she was doing at the time. That was admirable. My mother always said: patience and Lutz are two things that don't go together. It was patience that I learnt from Pina.

*The roles that you developed, did you try to bring something of yourself to them?*

That happens automatically. But nevertheless I still view them as 'roles'. I didn't experience everything myself. Some things you have seen elsewhere. Some things you work out for yourself. What's lovely is that the audience don't know the difference. At no time did I forget during all those rehearsals that what we are doing, we are doing for the stage. I had great trust in Pina. She never allowed a dancer to look bad.

She protected many dancers from themselves. There is a difference between the development process and the finished work. Only once it is staged and performed does it become a 'role' that I have made my mark on. Having performed several works for a long time now, some of them for over thirty years, this has been reinforced.

*Have you developed the roles over time?*

Yes, of course the pieces continue to develop. I am not the person today that I was back then. It was particularly exciting when *1980* was revived. I took over the revival of this piece in 2012 before I became artistic director. It was interesting to see how this piece changed simply because we were older and more mature. Many people who had seen it before said that it was actually more appropriate now. One notices that in getting older one becomes more sparing – you don't have the same stamina as you did thirty years ago – you also notice that previously you were doing far too much. That is an interesting process. The works are so complex and connected by so many memories. You carry a sort of photo album around in you. Not only of performances, but also encounters and experiences on tour. Such as when we were in Rome and Fellini came and paid me the loveliest compliment of my life: 'You are just like a clown, so sad and so funny.'

*What is it like for you to pass on the roles?*

Now it is easy; at the beginning it was harder. No dancer who succeeds you can do it right. If he doesn't do it well, you get annoyed that they're not making an effort. If he does it too well, that's not right either. However, for me, this phase is over now. Some of the pieces that I still perform, I perform in a reduced form; but in the meantime one thing has become clear: the 2015/16 season – which is my fortieth year with the Tanztheater – will be my last one as an active dancer.

*Is that a final goodbye?*

Yes, there's no going back. I used to think: if you can do it for ten years, then you'll be happy. Next year I will be sixty-three and I will have danced for forty-one years. I think it's lovely that it's possible to say goodbye slowly. It's essential. At some point with *Nelken* I thought, this isn't right any more. That was a young man. I didn't feel comfortable doing it anymore, and I'm not the type who hangs on to things.

*In 2013 you became artistic director of the company. What was the biggest challenge?*

Getting over the shock. There are things that I always wanted. I wanted to go to Wuppertal, I wanted to go to America, I wanted to teach at Folkwang. But I never wanted to be artistic director of the Tanztheater Wuppertal! When Pina died, this request was brought to my attention. I said: for heaven's sake, that's not for me. The only thing that convinced me was that the entire Tanztheater Wuppertal wanted it so. I'd be sitting around the table with everyone else. Or so I thought.

*You were to help prepare for the restructuring from 2016 onwards?*

Initially my job was different. The company was in a difficult position internally. From the start I thought sharing the leadership was not a happy solution, and it led to many problems. For me the first task was to create an atmosphere in which one could go back to concentrating on the work. And turn the animosities that had developed back into the joy of working. That took eighteen months. I first had to find out where the biggest problems were. Which also had something to do with the varying ages of the company. I had to see how things would continue with the repertoire. It was clear that it was only possible with new dancers. I'm for a fluent transition. That makes it all possible. And even if everyone was crying out for new work – which we will do in the future – I am of the opinion that it would not have been possible so early. The most important thing for me was that the company understood that we had to work with new choreographers. We are a multi-generational company, from twenty-four to sixty-four, like a large family. People have different life plans. It was my task to bring all that together.

*Is there a new orientation?*

The fact that the company has to make new work is as clear as day. But I would not describe that as a new orientation. New works belong to everyday life. But if it is to remain the Tanztheater Wuppertal Pina Bausch, then it will only do so if we continue to perform Pina's works. Maintaining the pieces is an active and creative process. It is not museum work. A complicated yet beautiful process, I think. It takes time. You can't just throw people in there, you have to let them grow into it. A Pina Bausch centre in the Schauspielhaus is a glorious idea. Maintaining the repertoire in an active and living form is essential.

*You believe it is possible to do old and new alongside each other?*

Yes, I believe that it is mutually enriching. Many of these works are masterpieces. The more I deal with it all from the outside, the more astonished I am sometimes and the more I admire Pina for what she did. Over the past two years we re-cast thirty to thirty-five parts. The astonishing thing is that it all works wonderfully. Of course some people say: it was so beautiful when you sang 'The Man I Love'. But, for heaven's sake! At some point it is over. And for those people who have never seen it, well, it's not a problem.

*Is one allowed to interfere with the works?*

No. Pina would have loved to have maintained all pieces. To do that, sometimes one has to resort to a couple of tricks – for example how she handed out the roles. I've also done something like that. Pina left behind a tool-box that one can make use of. But shortening the works, for example, we don't have the right to do that.

*What do you miss most about working with Pina Bausch on a daily basis?*

Pina. When I'm working, I try not to constantly think, what would she have done now? I don't think she would have wanted that. Pina once replied to a question from a journalist as to what advice she'd give a young dancer – 'None. Because everyone has to work it out for themselves.' And I can only hope that the thirty-four years that I worked with her have somehow left something behind which helps me in my daily life. But I do have to make decisions and I can't just sit there and think about what she might have done. In quieter moments, not during work, is when I think about her.

*And what is Pina Bausch's legacy?*

I hope it is humanity. Her theatre was a sensual experience, it was about feeling something and learning something about oneself. And I hope that that is her legacy.

**Lutz Förster,** born 1953 in Solingen, was engaged by Pina Bausch for the Tanztheater Wuppertal's production of *The Rite of Spring* in 1975 whilst he was still a student at the Folkwang-Hochschule in Essen. He became a permanent member of the ensemble in 1978 and distinguished himself as one of the most outstanding dancers and performers in the company. After a residential bursary in New York from 1981 to 1982, which he mainly spent as a dancer with the José Limón company, he returned to New York in from 1984–87 as acting artistic director of the Limón company. At the same time he remained closely tied to the Tanztheater: he rejoined Bausch's company on his return from the USA. Parallel to that he appeared in productions by Robert Wilson at the Hamburg State Theatre and at La Scala in Milan. In 1991 he took up a professorship at the Folkwang-Hochschule and ran the dance department as well as the Folkwang Tanzstudio until 2012 (jointly with Pina Bausch until her death in 2009). He continues to perform with the Tanztheater Wuppertal both at home and abroad, and in April 2013 became its artistic director.

# PINA BAUSCH BIOGRAPHY

27 July 1940   Philippine Bausch born in Solingen, attended the
Volksschule Ketzberg Solingen until 1955

1955-1959   Studied dance at the Folkwangschule, Essen. Left
with a Diploma in Stage Dance and Dance Pedagogy

1958   Won the Folkwang Prize for Achievement

1959   Began her studies at the Juilliard School of Music in
New York, during this period she was a dancer with
Paul Sansardo and Donya Feuer, was engaged at the
New American Ballet and at the Metropolitan Opera
House Ballet

1962   Returned to Essen and the Folkwang Hochschule,
member of the Folkwang Ballet

1969   Head of the Folkwang Tanzstudio; First prize at the
Second International Choreography Competition in
Cologne for 'Im Wind der Zeit'

1971   Guest choreography 'Aktionen für Tänzer' at the
Wuppertal Bühnen

Pina Bausch
accepts the
Eduard von
der Heydt-
Prize from
the City of
Wuppertal
in 1978
together with
her ensemble

| 1972 | Prize for Most Promising Young Artist from the state of North Rhine-Westphalia |
|------|---------------------------------------------------------------------------------|
| 1973 | Engagement at the Wuppertal Bühnen as Head of Ballet |
| 1974 | First premiere in Wuppertal: 'Fritz' |
| 1977 | First tour abroad, in Nancy and Vienna |
| 1978 | Eduard von der Heydt Prize from the city of Wuppertal |
| 1979 | Invitation to the Berlin Theatertreffen with 'Arien' |
| 1980 | Death of her set designer and partner Rolf Borzik on 27 January |
| 1981 | Birth of her son, Rolf Salomon, on 28 September. Lived from then on together with his father, Ronald Kay, in Wuppertal |
| 1983 | Took over as director of the dance department at the Folkwang Hochschule |
| 1984 | German Critic's Prize from the Verband der deutschen Kritiker at the Akademie der Künste, Berlin |
| 1986 | First Class Order of Merit of the Federal Republic of Germany, presented by the Federal President Richard von Wiezsäcker |
| 1987 | Four-week retrospective in Wuppertal with ten different Tanztheater pieces; Prize of the Dance Critics Society Japan |
| 1990 | Prize from the FRG Centre of the International Theatre Institute on the occasion of World Theatre Day 1990; NRW State Prize, presented by Johannes Rau, Governor of the state of North Rhine-Westphalia |

| 1991 | SACD Prize for Dance 1991 (Societé des Auteurs et Compositeurs dramatique); 'Rheinische Kulturpreis' from the Sparkassenstiftung zur Förderung rheinischen Kulturgutes, Düsseldorf; appointed as Commandeur de l'Ordre des Arts et des Lettres by the French Minister of Culture Jack Lang in Paris |
|------|---|
| 1993 | Pina Bausch hands over the directorship of the Folkwang Dance Department to Lutz Förster; UNESCO Picasso Medal |
| 1994 | Retrospective of thirteen pieces from the Tanztheater to celebrate twenty years part of the International Dance Festival NRW; awarded the Cruz da Ordem Militar de Santiago de España bestowed by the Portuguese State President Mário Suaraz |
| 1995 | German Dance Prize of the Deutscher Berufsverband für Tanzpädagogik e.V.; Joana Maria Gorvin Prize awarded by the Deutche Akademie der Schönen Künste in Berlin |
| 1997 | Berlin Theatre Prize; admission to the Order Pour le Mérite; Great Cross of the Order of Merit with Star and Shoulder Band of the Federal Republic of Germany; Ring of Honour from the city of Wuppertal |
| 1998 | 'Ein Fest in Wuppertal': Twenty-five years of Pina Bausch's Tanztheater; Bambi Award (for culture) |
| 1999 | Praemium Imperiale for Theatre and Film, conferred by the Japan Art Association, presented by Prince Hitachi; Honorary Doctorate (laurea honoris causa) of the University of Bologna in the fields of visual arts, music and theatre; European Theatre Prize |

| 2000 | Lifetime Achievement Award at the Istanbul Festival; Award of the International Association of Performing Arts |
| 2001 | 'Ein Fest in Wuppertal' |
| 2003 | Chevalier de l'Ordre National de la Légion d'Honneur, Paris; Spanish World Art Prize Valldigna |
| 2004 | International Dance Festival NRW under the directorship of Pina Bausch; Commander's Cross of the Order of Merit of the Republic of Italy; Nijinsky Award, Monte Carlo |
| 2005 | Golden Mask – Best Foreign Production, Golden Mask Festival of Performing Arts, Moscow; Honorary Ambassador for Culture and the Arts of the Republic of Korea |

Pina Bausch receives the Praemium Imperiale (1999) of the Japan Association from Prince Hitachi. It is the most highly-remunerated art prize in the world

| 2006 | Laurence Olivier Award, London, for 'Nelken'; Honorary Doctorate (laurea honoris causa) of the Juilliard School, New York; Direzione Onoraria of the Accademia Nazionale di Danza, Rome |
|------|------|
| 2007 | Orden al Mérito Artístico y Cultural 'Pablo Neruda' of the Consejo Nacional de la Cultura y las Artes de Chile, bestowed by the Chilean president Michelle Bachelet; Golden Lion at the Venice Biennale for Lifetime Achievement; Kyoto Prize in the category Art and Philosophy, bestowed by the Inamori Foundation, Kyoto |
| 2008 | International Dance Festival NRW under the directorship of Pina Bausch; Goethe Prize from the city of Frankfurt; Order of the Rising Sun on a Headband with Golden Rays from the Japanese Imperial House; Music Prize of the city of Duisburg; Honorary Citizen of the city of Wuppertal |
| 2009 | On 30 June Pina Bausch died in hospital in Wuppertal; her funeral at the Reformed Evangelical Cemetery in Wuppertal-Varresbeck was attended by a small circle of close friends; on 4 September memorial service took place at the opera house with 800 attendees; she was awarded the German theatre prize Der Faust posthumously for her lifetime achievement |

Pina Bausch links arms with Johannes Rau, Minister President of NRW at the time: the
Wuppertal Carnival Association awarded the choreographer the 1988 Order of Tolerance

# Books

Leonetta Bentivoglio and Francesco Carbone, "Pina Bausch oder Die Lust über Nelken zu tanzen", Suhrkamp Taschenbuch, 2007

"Café Müller – Ein Stück von Pina Bausch", Book and DVD, L'Arche and Arthaus Musik, 2010

Guy Delahaye, "Pina Bausch", Edition Braus, 2007

Jo Ann Endicott, "Warten auf Pina – Aufzeichnungen einer Tänzerin", Henschel Verlag, 2009

Jo Ann Endicott, "Ich bin eine anständige Frau", Suhrkamp Verlag, 2000

Raimund Hoghe, "Pina Bausch – Tanztheatergeschichten", Suhrkamp Verlag, 1986

"Kontakthof with Ladies and Gentlemen over 65", A piece by Pina Bausch Tanztheater Wuppertal, Book and DVD, L'Arche Verlag, 2007

Anne Linsel and Ulli Weiss, "Tanzträume. Jugendliche tanzen Kontakthof von Pina Bausch", Verlag HP Nacke, 2011

"Rolf Borzik und das Tanztheater", Hrsg. Tanztheater Wuppertal GmbH, 2000

Susanne Schlichter, "Tanztheater", Rowohlt Enzyklopädie, 1987

Jochen Schmidt, "Pina Bausch – Tanzen gegen die Angst", Econ Verlag, 1998

Norbert Servos, "Pina Bausch Tanztheater oder die Kunst einen Goldfisch zu zähmen", Kallmeyer Verlag

Norbert Servos, "Pina Bausch Tanztheater", K. Kieser Verlag, 2008

Patricia Stöckemann, "Etwas ganz Neues muß entstehen – Kurt Jooss und das Tanztheater", K. Kieser Verlag, 2001

"Pina Bausch – Fotografien von Detlef Erler", Edition Stemmle, Kirchberg/Zürich, 1994

Walter Vogel, "Pina", Quadriga Verlag, 1999

Wim Wenders and Peter Pabst, "Peter für/for/pour Pina– Die Bühnenbilder von Peter Pabst für die Stücke von Pina Bausch", Kettler, 2010

## Essays and Interviews:

"Ballett 1975", Chronik und Bilder der Ballettjahres, Friedrich Verlag, 1976

Conversation with Ruth Berghaus, 29 May 1987, Source: Archiv Tanztheater

GI Intern, a Goethe-Institut publication, 3/1998

Mechthild Großmann, "Ein Stück für Pina", Emma, Winter 2010

Interview Pina Bausch with Martina Wohlthat, Basler Zeitung, 18 September 2003

Interview Pina Bausch, in: Der Bund, Basel, 20 September 2003

Interview Pina Bausch, in: Tip, Berlin-Magazin, 2/1980

Interview Pina Bausch with Frank Scurla and Marion Meyer, Westdeutsche Zeitung, 10 Oktober 1998

Interview Pina Bausch with Christiane Gibiec, Frankfurter Rundschau, 17 October 1998

Interview Pina Bausch with Gert Gliewe, Münchner Abendzeitung, 22 May 1992

Interview Pina Bausch with Lothar Schmidt-Mühlisch, Die Welt, 5 May 2000

Interview Pina Bausch with Eva-Elisabeth Fischer, Süddeutsche Zeitung, 25/26 September 2004

Interview Pina Bausch with Ulrich Deuter and Andreas Wilink in K West, October 2004

Interview Peter Pabst with Marion Meyer, Westdeutsche Zeitung, 29 November 2008

Pina Bausch, "What moves me", Inamori Foundation, 2007, on the occasion of the Kyoto Prize awarded to Pina Bausch

Pina Bausch, "Etwas finden, was keiner Frage bedarf", Speech at the Kyoto Prize Workshop, Inamori Foundation, 2007

## Films:

"Damen und Herren ab 65", Film by Lilo Mangelsdorff, NDR/ Arte, 2002

"Das Tanztheater der Pina Bausch", Film by Christiane Gibiec for 25th anniversary of Tanztheater Wuppertal, WDR/ARD, 1998

"Nelken in Indien. Pina Bausch und ihr Tanztheater auf Tournee", Film by Anne Linsel, Arte, 1994

"Pina Bausch", Film by Anne Linsel, Tag/Traum-Filmproduktion/WDR/Arte, 2006

"Sir Arno – Der Theatermacher Arno Wüstenhöfer", Film by Claudia Gehre and Christiane Gibiec, WDR/ORB, 1994

"Tanzträume. Kontakthof mit Jugendlichen", Film by Anne Linsel and Rainer Hoffmann, Tag/Traum- Filmproduktion/ WDR/Arte, 2010

"Pina – tanzt, tanzt sonst sind wir verloren", Documentary film by Wim Wenders, Neue Road Movies, Germany/France, 2011

# FOOTNOTES

**Pina Bausch, An Introduction**

1. Raimund Hoghe, 'Pina Bausch', p. 106
2. Interview with Norbert Servos, 16 February 1990 in: Norbert Servos, 'Pina Bausch Tanztheater oder die Kunst einen Goldfisch zu zähmen', p. 305
3. As above, p. 306
4. Raimund Hoghe, 'Pina Bausch', p. 28
5. Interview with Frank Scurla and Marion Meyer, Westdeutsche Zeitung, 10 October 1998
6. See 2)
7. 'Pina Bausch – Fotografien von Detlef Erler', p. 19
8. Jo Ann Endicott, 'Warten auf Pina – Aufzeichnungen einer Tänzerin', p. 87
9. Jochen Schmidt, 'Pina Bausch – Tanzen gegen die Angst', p. 17
10. Interview with Norbert Servos, 13 September 1998, in: Norbert Servos, 'Pina Bausch Tanztheater', p. 265
11. 'Nelken in Indien. Pina Bausch und ihr Tantztheater auf Tournee', film by Anne Linsel, 1994

**Childhood and Adolescence**

1. Guy Delahaye, 'Pina Bausch', p. 13
2. Walter Vogel, 'Pina', p. 9
3. Pina Bausch, 'Was mich bewegt', Inamori Foundation, 2007

4. 'Ballett 1975', chronicle and photos of a year in ballet
5. See 3)
6. See 3)
7. Interview in: Tip, Berlin-Magazin, 2/1980
8. Interview with Jochen Schmidt, 9 November 1978, in: Norbert Servos, 'Pina Basch oder die Kunst einen Goldfisch zu zähmen', p. 262
9. See 3)
10. See 8)
11. See 3)
12. Pina Bausch, 'Etwas finden, was keiner Frage bedarf', Speech at the Kyoto Prize Workshop, Inamori Foundation, 2007
13. Patricia Stöckemann, 'Etwas ganz Neues muβ entstehen – Kurt Jooss und das Tanztheater', p. 364
14. Interview with Jean-Marc Adolphe on 1 March 2006, in: Guy Delahaye, 'Pina Bausch', p. 26
15. See 3)
16. As above
17. See 2) p. 14
18. See 12)
19. See 2) p. 41
20. See 2) p. 38
21. See 2) p. 26
22. See 2) p. 25

**From New York to Essen**

1. Patricia Stöckemann, 'Etwas ganz Neues muβ entstehen – Kurt Jooss und das Tanztheater', p. 365
2. Pina Bausch, 'Was mich bewegt', Inamori Foundation, 2007
3. Interview with Jochen Schmidt, 9 November 1978, in: Norbert Servos, 'Pina Bausch oder die Kunst einen Goldfisch zu zähmen', p. 262
4. As above, p. 263
5. Interview with Jean-Marc Adolphe on 1 March 2006, in: Guy Delahaye, 'Pina Bausch', p. 27
6. As above p. 29
7. As above p. 28
8. Walter Vogel, 'Pina', p. 19
9. Pina Bausch, 'Was mich bewegt', Inamori Foundation, 2007
10. See 5) p. 29
11. As above p. 30
12. Jochen Schmidt, 'Pina Bausch – Tanzen gegen die Angst', p. 33
13. Interview with Christiane Gibiec, Frankfurter Rundschau, 17 October 1998
14. See 3) p. 292
15. See 13)
16. Interview in the Münchner Abenzeitung, 22 May 1992

**Beginnings in Wuppertal**

1. 'Sir Arno – Der Theatermacher Arno Wüstenhöfer', film by Claudia Gehre and Christiane Gibiec, 1994

2. 'Das Tanztheater der Pina Bausch', 1998, film by Christian Gibiec
3. See 1)
4. Susanne Schlichter, 'Tanztheater', p. 108
5. 'Pina Bausch', film by Anne Linsel, 2006
6. As above
7. Interview with Jean-Marc Adolphe on 1 March 2006, in: Guy Delahaye, 'Pina Bausch', p. 30
8. As above, p. 31
9. 'Die Zeit', 1 February 1974
10. Abendzeitung München, 10 January 1974
11. See 7) p. 31
12. As above
13. Pina Bausch: 'Was mich bewegt', Inamori Foundation, 2007
14. As above
15. 15) FAZ, 3 June 1975
16. See 7) p. 32

**Breaking away to create new forms**

1. WAZ, 10 December 1974
2. Rheinische Post, 24 June 1976
3. Interview with Norbert Servos, 30 December 1995, in Norbert Servos: 'Pina Basch oder die Kunst einen Goldfisch zu zähmen', pp. 307-308
4. Die Welt, 10 January 1977
5. Interview with Lothar Schmidt-Mühlisch, Die Welt, 5 May 2000
6. Interview with Andreas Wilink and Ulrich Deuter in K.West, October 2004
7. 'Pina Bausch', film by Anne Linsel, 2006

**Kontakthof**

1. 'Kontakthof with Ladies and Gentlemen over 65', Book and DVD, p. 38
2. As above
3. 'Tanzträume. Kontakthof mit Jugendlichen', film by Anne Linsel, 2010

**The Working Process**

1. Interview with Jochen Schmidt, 26 November 1982, in: Norbert Servos, 'Pina Bausch oder die Kunst einen Goldfisch zu zähmen', p. 299
2. Pina Bausch: 'Was mich bewegt', Inamori Foundation, 2007
3. Raimund Hoghe, 'Pina Bausch', p. 109
4. Leonetta Bentivoglio and Francesco Carbone, 'Pina Bausch oder Die Lust über Nelken zu tanzen', p. 63
5. Jo Ann Endicott, 'Warten auf Pina', p. 80
6. Conversation with Ruth Berghaus, 29 May 1987, source: Tanztheater archive
7. Interview with Lothar Schmidt Mühlisch, die Welt, 5 May 2000
8. As above
9. Interview with Eva-Elisabeth Fischer, Süddeutsche Zeitung, 25/26 September 2004
10. See 3) p. 40
11. Interview with Andreas Wilink and Ulrich Deuter in K.West, October 2004
12. Pina Bausch, 'Etwas finden, was keiner Frage bedarf', Inamori Foundation, 2007

13. Interview with Norbert Servos, 13 September 1998 in Norbert Servos: 'Pina Bausch Tanztheater', p. 263
14. Interview with Norbert Servos, 16 February 1990 in: Norbert Servos, 'Pina Bausch oder die Kunst einen Goldfisch zu zähmen', p. 304
15. See 9)
16. See 3) p. 117
17. See 13) p. 263

**How the Works are Created**

1. 'Pina Bausch', film by Anne Linsel, 2006
2. Conversations with Ruth Berghaus, 29 May 1987, source: Tanztheater archive
3. See 1)
4. See 2)
5. GI intern, the Goethe-Institut paper, 3/1998
6. Interview with Norbert Servos, 13 September 1998 in Norbert Servos: 'Pina Bausch Tanztheater', p. 261
7. See 1)
8. See 5)
9. Raimund Hoghe, 'Pina Bausch', pp. 15/18
10. Pina Bausch, 'Etwas finden, was keiner Frage bedarf', Inamori Foundation, 2007

**Premieres and Re-rehearsals**

1. Interview with Lothar Schmidt-Mühlisch, Die Welt, 5 May 2000
2. As above

3. Interview with Jochen Schmidt, 26 November 1982, in: Norbert Servos, 'Pina Bausch oder die Kunst einen Goldfisch zu zähmen', p. 301
4. As above, p. 296
5. Interview with Norbert Servos, 13 September 1998 in Norbert Servos: 'Pina Bausch Tanztheater', p. 252
6. Interview with Ruth Berhaus, 29 May 1987, source: Tanztheater archive
7. Interview with Norbert Servos, 16 February 1990 in: Norbert Servos, 'Pina Bausch oder die Kunst einen Goldfisch zu zähmen', p. 304
8. See 6)

**Private Turmoil and Classics of the Tanztheater**

1. Pina Bausch: 'Was mich bewegt', Inamori Foundation, 2007
2. Interview with Jochen Schmidt, 21 April 1982, in: Norbert Servos, 'Pina Bausch oder die Kunst einen Goldfisch zu zähmen', p. 296
3. Pina Bausch: 'Was mich bewegt', Inamori Foundation, 2007
4. Interview with Jochen Schmidt, 23 December 1983, in: Norbert Servos, 'Pina Bausch oder die Kunst einen Goldfisch zu zähmen', p. 296

**Wuppertal on the Road**

1. Interview with Jochen Schmidt, 26 November 1982, in: Norbert Servos, 'Pina Bausch oder die Kunst einen Goldfisch zu zähmen', p. 297
2. Interview with Andreas Wilink and Ulrich Deuter in K.West, October 2004
3. Interview in the Basler Zeitung, 18 September 2003
4. 'Das Tanztheater der Pina Bausch', film by Christiane Gibiec, 1998
5. Interview with Norbert Servos, 16 February 1990, in: Norbert Servos, 'Pina Bausch oder die Kunst einen Goldfisch zu zähmen', p. 306
6. See 4)
7. See 1) p. 300
8. See 2)
9. 'Pina Bausch', film by Anne Linsel, 2006
10. Interview with Christiane Gibiec, Frankfurter Rundschau, 17 October 1998
11. See 2)

**The Era of Co-productions**

1. Pina Bausch: 'Was mich bewegt,' Inamori Foundation, 2007
2. As above
3. As above

**The Ensemble**

1. 'Pina Bausch', film by Anne Linsel, 2006
2. Interview in: Der Bund, Basel, 20 September 2003

3.  Pina Bausch, 'Etwas finden, was keiner Frage bedarf', Inamori Foundation, 2007
4.  Mechthild Großmann, 'Ein Stück für Pina', Emma, Winter 2010
5.  As above
6.  'Pina', film by Wim Wenders, 2011
7.  As above
8.  Interview with Christiane Gibiec, Frankfurter Rundschau, 17 October 1998
9.  'Das Tanztheater der Pina Bausch', film by Christiane Gibiec, 1998
10. See 6)
11. Pina Bausch: 'Was mich bewegt', Inamori Foundation, 2007
12. Interview with Jean-Marc Adophe, 1 March 2006, in: Guy Delahaye, 'Pina Bausch', p. 38
13. Jo Ann Endicott, 'Warten auf Pina', p. 14
14. See 1)
15. Interview with Eva-Elisabeth Fischer, Süddeutsche Zeitung, 25/26 September 2004
16. Jo Ann Endicott, 'Ich bin eine anständige Frau', p. 133
17. See 4)

**The Set Designers**

1.  Interview with Marion Meyer, Westdeutsche Zeitung, 29 November 2008
2.  Pina Bausch, 'Etwas finden, was keiner Frage bedarf', Inamori Foundation, 2007

3.  Wim Wenders and Peter Pabst, 'Peter für/for/pour Pina – Die Bühnenbilder von Peter Pabst für die Stücke von Pina Bausch', p. 4
4.  As above, p. 25
5.  Interview with Norbert Servos, 15 October 2007, in: Norbert Servos, 'Pina Bausch Tanztheater', p. 277
6.  See 1)
7.  See 1)
8.  See 3) p. 27
9.  See 3 p. 29

**The Costumes**

1.  Interview with Norbert Servos, 30 September 1995, in: Norbert Servos, 'Pina Bausch oder die Kunst einen Goldfisch zu zähmen', p. 296
2.  Interview with Norbert Servos, 1 November 2007, in: Norbert Servos, 'Pina Bausch Tanztheater', p. 270
3.  As above, p. 272

**The Music**

1.  All quotes from a conversation between the author and Matthias Burkert, 2 August 2011
2.  Interview with Norbert Servos, 20 September 1995, in: Norbert Servos, 'Pina Bausch oder die Kunst einen Goldfisch zu zähmen', p. 296

# WORKS

*1973*
**Fritz**
Dance-evening by Pina Bausch
Music: Gustav Mahler, Wolfgang Hufschmidt
In the same programme: "Der grüne Tisch" by Kurt Jooss and "Rodeo" by
Agnes de Mille
**Iphigenie auf Tauris**
Dance-opera by Pina Bausch Music: Christoph W. Gluck

*1974*
**Ich bring' dich um die Ecke**
Pop music ballet by Pina Bausch
**Adagio**
by Pina Bausch

*1975*
**Orpheus und Eurydike**
Dance-opera by Pina Bausch
Music: Christoph W. Gluck
**Frühlingsopfer**
**Wind von West**
**Der zweite Frühling**
**Le Sacre du Printemps**
by Pina Bausch
Music: Igor Stravinsky

*1976*
**Die sieben Todsünden**
Die sieben Todsünden der Kleinbürger / Fürchtet Euch nicht
Dance-evening by Pina Bausch
Musik: Kurt Weill, Texte: Bertolt Brecht

*1977*
**Blaubart – beim Anhören einer Tonbandaufnahme von Béla Bartóks "Herzog**
**Blaubarts Burg"**
A piece by Pina Bausch
**Komm tanz mit mir**
A piece by Pina Bausch
**Renate wandert aus**
An operetta by Pina Bausch

*1978*

**Er nimmt sie an der Hand und führt sie in das**
**Schloss, die anderen folgen …**
A piece by Pina Bausch
A co-production with Schauspielhaus Bochum
**Café Müller**
A piece by Pina Bausch
**Kontakthof**
A piece by Pina Bausch

*1979*
**Arien**
A piece by Pina Bausch
**Keuschheitslegende**
A piece by Pina Bausch

*1980*
**1980 – A piece by Pina Bausch**

*1981*
**Bandoneon**
A piece by Pina Bausch

*1982*
**Walzer**
A piece by Pina Bausch
In co-production with the Holland Festival
**Nelken**
A piece by Pina Bausch

*1984*
**Auf dem Gebirge hat man ein Geschrei gehört**
A piece by Pina Bausch

*1985*
**Two Cigarettes in the Dark**
A piece by Pina Bausch

*1986*
**Viktor**
A piece by Pina Bausch
In co-production with Teatro Argentina and the City of Rome

*1987*

**Ahnen**

A piece by Pina Bausch

*1989*

**Palermo Palermo**

A piece by Pina Bausch

In co-production with Teatro Biondo, Palermo and Andres Neumann

International

*1990*

**Die Klage der Kaiserin**

A film for cinema by Pina Bausch

*1991*

**Tanzabend II**

A piece by Pina Bausch

In co-production with the Festival de Otoño, Madrid

*1993*

**Das Stück mit dem Schiff**

A piece by Pina Bausch

*1994*

**Ein Trauerspiel**

A piece by Pina Bausch

In co-production with the Wiener Festwochen

*1995*

**Danzón**

A piece by Pina Bausch

*1996*

**Nur Du**

A piece by Pina Bausch

In co-production with the University of California in Los Angeles,
the Arizona State University, the University of California in Berkley, the
University of Texas in Austin and Darlene Neel Presentations and Rena
Shagan Associates, Inc. and The Music Center Inc.

*1997*

**Der Fensterputzer**
A piece by Pina Bausch
In co-production with the Hong Kong Arts Festival
Society and the Goethe-Institut Hong Kong

*1998*
**Masurca Fogo**
A piece by Pina Bausch
In co-production with EXPO 98 Lisbon and the
Goethe-Institut Lisbon

*1999*
**O Dido**
A piece by Pina Bausch
In co-production with Teatro Argentina in Rome and Andres Neumann
International

*2000*
**Kontakthof – Mit Damen und Herren ab "65"**
A piece by Pina Bausch
**Wiesenland**
A piece by Pina Bausch
In co-production with the Goethe-Institut Budapest and Théâtre de la Ville Paris

*2001*
**Água**
A piece by Pina Bausch
In co-production with Brazil, the Goethe-Institut
Sao Paulo and Emilio Kalil

*2002*
**Für die Kinder von gestern, heute und morgen**
A piece by Pina Bausch

*2003*
**Nefés**
A piece by Pina Bausch
In co-production with the International Istanbul Theatre Festival and the
Istanbul Foundation of Culture and Arts

*2004*
**Ten Chi**
A piece by Pina Bausch
In co-production with the Saitama Prefecture, Saitama
Arts Foundation and Nippon Cultural Center

*2005*
**Rough Cut**
A piece by Pina Bausch
In co-production with the LG Arts Center and the
Goethe-Institut Seoul, Korea

*2006*
**Vollmond**
A piece by Pina Bausch

*2007*
**Bamboo Blues**
A piece by Pina Bausch
In co-production with the Goethe-Instituts of India

*2008*
**Sweet Mambo**
A piece by Pina Bausch
**Kontakthof – Mit Teenagern ab "14"**
A piece by Pina Bausch

*2009*
**"…como el musguito en la piedra, ay si, si, si …"**
In co-production with the Festival Internacional de Teatro Santiago a Mil
in Chile and with the support of the Goethe-Institut Chile
In co-production with Andres Neumann International

# INDEX

# IMAGE CREDITS

# MARION MEYER BIOGRAPHY

Marion Meyer, born 1966 in Wuppertal, studied German and English Studies and worked as an assistant director in theatre initially in Wuppertal and then in Bochum. For fourteen years she was the editor of a daily newspaper, becoming a self-employed journalist in 2010. Since 2013 she has been looking after press and PR for the Von der Heydt Museum in Wuppertal.

I would like to thank everyone who supported me with the writing of this book: Tanztheater Wuppertal, above all Ursula Popp, Grigori Chakhov, Marc Wagenbach and Claudia Irman, who made the archive and film recordings available to me at all times, and who provided plenty of food for thought. I would also like to thank my husband Jörg Isringhaus, Prof. Renate de Jong-Meyer and Christiane Gibiec for their patient revisions and constructive criticism.